APPLIED HARMONY

By GEORGE A. WEDGE

Book I: Diatonic Harmony

All human beings have, to a varying degree, the same fundamental equipment for the understanding of musical sound, rhythm and form—the three factors in musical expression. The composer uses this equipment as a skeleton around which he weaves the expression of his thoughts and emotions. He displays his genius and individuality through the manner in which this is done.

An understanding and appreciation of music can be developed through the study of the methods used by composers. This study should be approached through the ear. The purpose of this book is to furnish material with definite suggestions for study.

This work has been successfully presented in two one-hour classes a week, one hour for drill and dictation to groups of sixty to ninety students, and one hour for the correction of exercises and additional drill to groups of eight to ten students.

Price, net, $2.00 EC
(In U.S.A.)

G. SCHIRMER (INC.)

3 East 43rd Street :: :: :: :: New York

APPLIED HARMONY

A Text-book

By

GEORGE A. WEDGE

Book I — Diatonic

G. SCHIRMER (INC.)
NEW YORK

Printed in the U. S. A.

ACKNOWLEDGMENT

I wish to express most sincere gratitude to my friend, Dr. Frank Damrosch, who has made it possible to develop this work in the classes of the Institute of Musical Art of the Juilliard School of Music, New York City.

To my colleagues who have assisted me with untiring devotion, understanding and enthusiasm in its presentation.

To Miss Helen W. Whiley, Mrs. Sylvia Boardman, Mr. Howard Brockway, Mr. Howard A. Murphy and Mr. Howard Talley for suggestions and assistance in the preparation of the material and the manuscript.

GEORGE A. WEDGE.

PREFACE

Music is comprehended only through the ear. The symbols on a page of printed music are the directions for performance upon an instrument producing musical sounds.

All human beings have, to a varying degree, the same fundamental equipment for the understanding of musical sound, rhythm and form—the three factors in musical expression. The composer uses this equipment as a skeleton around which he weaves the expression of his thoughts and emotions. He displays his genius and individuality through the manner in which this is done.

An understanding and appreciation of music can be developed through the study of the methods used by composers. This study should be approached through the ear. The purpose of this book is to furnish material with definite suggestions for study.

The following plan is used in the drills:

Exercises for the mechanics of voice-leading in four-part vocal harmony.

Exercises for the use of a definite harmonic progression in relation to other chords, and its use in phrase and period forms.

Additional drill using this material in figured basses and melody harmonization.

Exercises for the use of this material in writing for the piano.

The study of form through the harmonization of melodies with piano accompaniment, the analysis of piano compositions, and the writing of original compositions.

The material of Sections (1), (2), (3), also one exercise of Section (4), is to be dictated in class. One exercise from each of the other sections will provide an ample assignment.

This work has been successfully presented in two one-hour classes a week, one hour for drill and dictation to groups of sixty to ninety students, and one hour for the correction of exercises and additional drill to groups of eight to ten students.

TABLE OF CONTENTS

[v]

CONTENTS

CONTENTS

CONTENTS

INHARMONIC TONES

PART III. APPLICATION IN FORM

APPLIED HARMONY

CHAPTER I—INTRODUCTORY

KEY AND SCALE

All art-forms have a basis from which they develop.

Music, no matter what system used or how obscure its meaning, must have such a basis if it is an artistic expression.

Music which uses the accepted (tempered) major and minor system has tonality as a basis, and is said to be written in a key.

A **key** is a series of seven related tones that are derived from a given tone in the following manner:

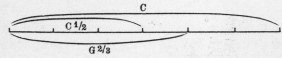

Given a string that vibrates to give the pitch in Middle C, to find the tone most nearly related in vibrations but different in sound, first divide the string in half. It will be found that each segment will vibrate twice as fast and the sound of each segment will still be C, but an octave higher.

Using the next ratio, thirds, divide the string into 3rds and set the large segment to vibrating and it will produce the tone G, a perfect 5th above C. Therefore, the nearest related tone to any tone and differing in pitch will be a 5th above.

Continuing this experiment, using middle C as a center, the following tones will be obtained:

Working conversely, i.e., measuring down in 5ths, the following tones will be obtained:

A choice of the tones of a key was made from this series of 5ths. Using any tone as a key-center, the first five tones above and the first tone below were selected. How this choice was made is not definitely known, but it was obviously influenced by the arrangement of the tones in the modal scales, by the distri-

[1]

bution of tones among the consonant overtones, and by the tones which meet the requirements of the tempered tuning of the modern piano keyboard.

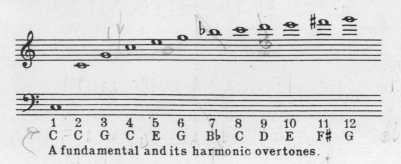

1	2	3	4	5	6	7	8	9	10	11	12
C	C	G	C	E	G	B♭	C	D	E	F♯	G

A fundamental and its harmonic overtones.

If C is the key-tone, the tones used are G, D, A, E and B above and F below; if G is the key-tone, the tones used are D, A, E, B and F♯ above and C below, etc.

A **major scale** is the arrangement of these tones upon the staff in consecutive order.

The Scale of C-major   The Scale of G-major

The **harmonic minor scale** is found by lowering one half-step the 3rd and 6th degrees of the major scale.

The other forms of the minor scale are: the **natural** or **Aeolian minor scale** which has a lowered 3rd, 6th and 7th degree.

The **ascending melodic minor scale** which has only the lowered 3rd degree.

The **descending melodic minor scale** is the same as the natural minor scale.

INTERVALS

Lesson I

The difference in pitch between two tones is an **interval.**

When the two tones are played or sung simultaneously the interval is harmonic.

When the two tones are played or sung one after the other the interval is melodic.

Only harmonic intervals are used in harmony.

Intervals are named and measured from the distance at which the tones are placed upon the staff. The lower tone of the interval is counted as 1. This is necessary because music is heard, not seen, and when an interval is heard the sound of each tone must be thought in measuring the difference in pitch. The notation is a representation of the sounds heard. Therefore, when this interval is heard and the sound visualized upon the staff, the lower tone is counted as 1 and each successive line and space as a degree. This interval is a 6th.

Two notes on the same line or in the same space which are to be played or sung at the same time by two violins or two singers are called the interval of a unison or a prime.

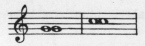

The distance from a line to the next space above or from a space to the next line above is a 2nd.

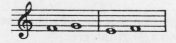

If the lower note of an interval is on a line the distance to the
first line above is a 3rd
second line above is a 5th
third line above is a 7th
fourth line above is a 9th;

the distance to the first space above is a 2nd
second space above is a 4th
third space above is a 6th
fourth space above is an 8ve
fifth space above is a 10th.

Similarly, *if the lower note of an interval is in a space* the distance to the
first space above is a 3rd
second space above is a 5th
third space above is a 7th
fourth space above is a 9th;

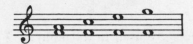

the distance to the first line above is a 2nd
second line above is a 4th
third line above is a 6th
fourth line above is an 8ve
fifth line above is a 10th.

Drill 1

(1) Write 3rds from each line and space on the staff without clef and from the leger-line above and below.

> In the same manner, write 5ths, 7ths and 9ths.
>
> Write a 2nd from each line and space of the staff and from the leger-line above and below.
>
> In the same manner write 4ths, 6ths, 8ves and 10ths.

(2) Write a 5th
      2nd
      7th
      3rd } from the 2nd line;
      8ve } from the 1st space below.
      4th
      6th

(3) Write a 9th
      3rd
      6th
      2nd { from the 1st leger-line below;
      5th { from the 2nd space below.
      7th
      4th
      8ve

(**4**) Using the G-clef write a 3rd
6th
2nd
4th
7th } from F, B, D, G, A, E, C.
5th
8ve
9th

(**5**) Using the F-clef write a 10th
2nd
5th
3rd } from D, B, G, F, C, E, A.
6th
4th
8ve
7th

TEACHER'S NOTE. There is no mention of scale or quality in this lesson. This is drill for spacing on the staff. Much of this drill should be given in class orally and in written form.

LESSON II

Intervals and chords are consonant or dissonant in sound.

A **consonant** sound is complete (i.e., satisfies the ear) and does not need resolution. This is caused by the nearness of the mathematical ratio of the vibrations of the two tones forming the interval; i. e., the 8ve, 2:1, the 5th, 3:2, the 4th, 4:3, etc. (See any book on physics.)

A **dissonant** sound is incomplete and needs resolution to a consonant sound. The ratio for these tones is greater; i.e., a second is 9:8, a seventh is 16:9, etc.

If the sound of the intervals of the preceding lesson is tested it will be found that the unisons, 3rds, 6ths, 8ths, 10ths and all of the 4ths and 5ths except F-B and B-F are consonant. The 2nds, 7ths and 9ths, also the 4th from F-B and the 5th from B-F are dissonant.

Testing all the 2nds on the staff (the white keys on the piano) it will be found that there are two sizes. The 2nd from E-F and from B-C is only one-half tone; all the other 2nds are whole tones.

Both kinds are dissonant.

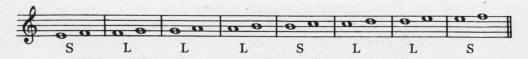

The 3rds are of two sizes, one one-half tone larger than the other. Both kinds are consonant.

All the 4ths are the same size except the 4th from F-B which is one-half tone larger.   All of the 4ths are consonant except the larger 4th which is dissonant.

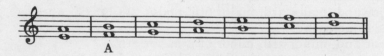

A

All the 5ths are the same size except the 5th from B-F which is one-half tone smaller.   All of the 5ths are consonant except the smaller 5th which is dissonant.

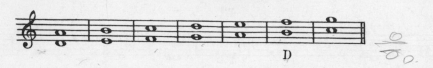

D

The 6ths are of two sizes, one one-half tone larger than the other.   Both kinds are consonant.

L   L   S   L   L   S   S

The 7ths are of two sizes, one one-half tone larger than the other.   Both kinds are dissonant.

L   S   S   L   S   S   S

The 8ves are all the same size and are consonant.

The 9ths and 10ths are the same as the 2nds and 3rds.

From the above testing it is clear that both sizes of 3rds and 6ths are consonant.   Also, that both sizes of 2nds and 7ths are dissonant.   The larger intervals are called **major** (large), the smaller intervals **minor** (small).   Therefore we have major or large 2nds, 3rds, 6ths and 7ths, and minor or small 2nds, 3rds, 6ths and 7ths.

The 4th which was larger and the 5th which was smaller were dissonant. It will be found later that if the 8ve and the prime are made larger or smaller with an accidental they become dissonant.   These consonant intervals which become dissonant when their size is altered are called **perfect** intervals.   Therefore there are perfect primes, 8ves, 5ths and 4ths.

The following table will be helpful in learning the names of these intervals as they appear upon the staff:

All of the 8ves and primes are perfect.

All the 2nds are major but E-F and B-C; these are minor.

The major 3rds are from C, F and G; the others are minor.

All 4ths are perfect except F-B.

All 5ths are perfect except B-F.

The major 6ths are from C, D, F and G; the others are minor.

The major 7ths are from C and F; the others are minor.

Drill 2

(1) As the quality name is always used in speaking of intervals, recite the following many times and in varied order:

Major 2nd, major 3rd, major 6th, major 7th.

Do the same with:

Minor 2nd, minor 3rd, minor 6th, minor 7th.

Also perfect prime, perfect 4th, perfect 5th, perfect 8ve.

(2) Learn the table of intervals given in this lesson.

(3) Name the intervals written in the preceding lesson.

(4) Name the following intervals:

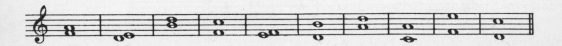

Lesson III

The size of any interval may be changed by altering the pitch of either the upper or lower tone by an accidental placed before the note or placed in the signature at the beginning of the staff.

When the upper tone is lowered the interval is smaller.
When the lower tone is raised the interval is smaller.

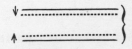

When the upper tone is raised the interval is larger.
When the lower tone is lowered the interval is larger.

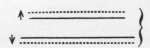

When both tones are raised or lowered the same distance the size of the interval is the same.

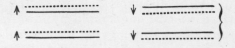

Any interval which is major upon the staff becomes minor when made one half-step smaller by an accidental or signature. Any interval which is minor upon the staff becomes major when made one half-step larger by an accidental or signature.

Drill 3

(1) Make all the major 3rds upon the staff minor by lowering the upper tone one half-step.

Make all the major 3rds upon the staff minor by raising the lower tone one half-step.

(2) Make all the minor 3rds upon the staff major by raising the upper tone one half-step.

Make all the minor 3rds upon the staff major by lowering the lower tone one half-step.

(3) Do the same with the major and minor 2nds, 6ths and 7ths.

(4) Alter the pitch of both tones of all intervals but leave the size of the interval unchanged.

(5) To each of the following intervals apply four key-signatures which will alter the size of the interval. Name each interval; e.g.

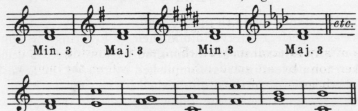

(6) Name the following intervals:

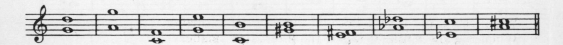

LESSON IV

All of the 4ths on the staff except the 4th from F-B are perfect. The 4th from F-B, which is one half-tone larger than the other fourths, is called **augmented.**

Each perfect interval may be augmented by raising the upper tone one half-step or lowering the lower tone one half-step.

Each major interval may be made one half-step larger in the same way and is then called augmented.

Augmented intervals are dissonant.

Drill 4

(1) Learn the augmented 4th on the staff.
(2) Make each perfect interval augmented by raising the upper tone.
(3) Make each major interval augmented by raising the upper tone.
(4) Make each perfect interval augmented by lowering the lower tone.
(5) Make each major interval augmented by lowering the lower tone.
(6) Apply key-signatures to the following intervals and name each interval, as in Drill 3:

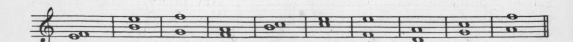

(7) Name the following intervals:

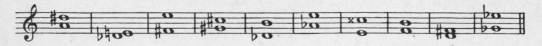

LESSON V

All the 5ths on the staff except B-F are perfect. This 5th is one half-tone smaller and is called **diminished.**

Each perfect interval may be diminished by lowering the upper tone one half-step or raising the lower tone one half-step.

Each minor interval may be diminished in the same manner.

Diminished intervals are dissonant. *except*

Drill 5

(1) Learn the diminished 5th on the staff.

(2) Make each perfect interval diminished by lowering the upper tone.

(3) Make each minor interval diminished by lowering the upper tone.

(4) Make each perfect interval diminished by raising the lower tone.

(5) Make each minor interval diminished by raising the lower tone.

(6) Apply key-signatures to the following intervals and name each interval, as in Drill 3:

(7) Name the following intervals:

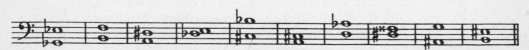

LESSON VI

An interval is **inverted** by placing the lower tone one octave higher. Upon inversion:

A 2nd becomes a 7th and the reverse (i.e., a 7th becomes a 2nd).

A 3rd becomes a 6th and the reverse.

A 4th becomes a 5th and the reverse.

Also

A major interval becomes minor and the reverse.

A diminished interval becomes augmented and the reverse.

A perfect interval remains perfect.

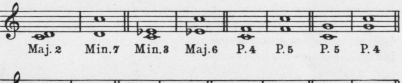

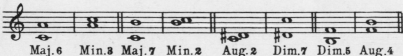

Drill 6

(1) Learn the table given above.
(2) Invert and name the following intervals:

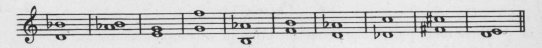

LESSON VII

An interval which is one whole tone larger than a perfect interval is **doubly augmented.**

An interval which is one whole tone smaller than a perfect interval is **doubly diminished.**

The most commonly used are the doubly diminished 5th and the doubly augmented 4th.

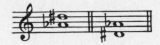

As the notes on the staff and the notes of the C-major scale are the same, the following table of intervals found between scale degrees will result. (This table will apply to each major scale):

Major 2nds all but 3–4, 7–8; these are minor.
Major 3rds from 1, 4 and 5; the others are minor.
Perfect 4ths all but 4–7, which is augmented.
Perfect 5ths all but 7–4 ,which is diminished.
Major 6ths from 1, 2, 4, 5; the others are minor.
Major 7ths from 1 and 4; the others are minor.

The following augmented and diminished intervals are peculiar to the minor scale:

Augmented 4th 6–2.
Diminished 5th 2–6.
Augmented 2nd 6–7.
Diminished 7th 7–6.
Augmented 5th 3–7.
Diminished 4th 7–3.

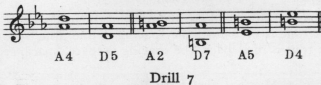

A 4   D 5   A 2   D 7   A 5   D 4

Drill 7

(1) Learn the tables given above.
(2) Name the following intervals:

CHAPTER III—Introductory
TRIADS
Lesson I

Three tones placed one above the other in 3rds form a **chord**.

A three-tone chord is called a **triad**.

Triads may be built from any tone.

The tone upon which the triad is built is the **root**. The first tone above the root is the **3rd** of the triad, the other tone is the **5th** of the triad.

When the root of a triad is on a line, the other tones are also on lines; when the root is in a space, the other tones are in spaces. In other words, the spacing of a triad is either line, line, line or space, space, space.

Triads are named from the letter-name of the root: e.g., a triad built upon E is the E triad, upon F the F triad, etc.

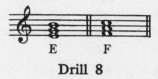

E   F

Drill 8

(1) Build a triad from each line and space of the G-staff, and upon the two leger-lines and spaces below the staff.

(2) Learn to spell triads from each letter-name; i.e., C-E-G, D-F-A, etc.

Lesson II

A triad is inverted when either its 3rd or 5th is on the bottom.

A triad is in the **first inversion** when its 3rd is on the bottom, the root on top.

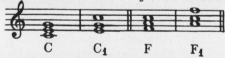

C C_1 F F_1

The inversion does not change the name of the triad. The illustration above is the C triad and the C triad in the first inversion, the F triad and the F triad in the first inversion.

The tones of a first inversion are arranged in the intervals of a 3rd and a 4th. When the lowest tone is on a line, the spacing is line, line, second space above. When the lowest tone is in a space, the spacing is space, space, second line above.

Drill 9

(1) Recite each triad, then its first inversion: e.g., C-E-G, E-G-C, D-F-A, F-A-D, etc. Visualize each as you recite.

(2) Learn to spell first inversions from each letter; e.g., E-G-C, F-A-D, etc.

(3) Write first inversions of triads from each line and space of the G-staff and the two leger-lines and spaces below.

Lesson III

A triad is in the **second inversion** when the 5th is on the bottom and the 3rd is on top.

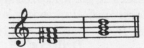

The illustration is a fundamental C triad and its second inversion.

The tones of a second inversion are arranged in the intervals of a 4th and a 3rd. When the lowest tone is on a line, the spacing is second space above, space above. When the lowest tone is in a space, the spacing is second line above, line above.

Drill 10

(1) Recite each triad, then its second inversion; e.g., C-E-G, G-C-E. Visualize each as you recite.

(2) Learn to spell second inversions from each letter; e.g., C-F-A, D-G-B, etc.

(3) Recite each triad, then its first inversion and second inversion.

(4) Write second inversions of triads from each line and space of the G-staff and the two leger-lines and spaces below.

(5) Write a triad from each letter followed by its second inversion.

Lesson IV

The quality of a triad is determined by the size of its 3rd and 5th.

A triad with a major 3rd and a perfect 5th is a **major triad.**

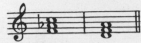

Drill 11

(1) Erect a major triad from each line and space of the G- and F-staffs.

(2) Erect a major triad from C♯, D♭, E♭, F♯, G♭, A♭, B♭.

Lesson V

A triad with a minor 3rd and a perfect 5th is a **minor triad.**

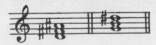

Major and minor triads are consonant.

Drill 12

(1) Erect a minor triad from each line and space of the G- and F-staffs.

(2) Erect a minor triad from each chromatic tone.

Lesson VI

A triad with a major 3rd and an augmented 5th is an **augmented triad.**

Drill 13

(1) Erect an augmented triad from each line and space of the G- and F-staffs.
(2) Erect an augmented triad from each chromatic tone.

LESSON VII

A triad with a minor 3rd and a diminished 5th is a **diminished triad.**

Augmented and diminished triads are dissonant.

Drill 14

(1) Erect a diminished triad from each line and space of the G- and F-staffs.
(2) Erect a diminished triad from each chromatic tone.

LESSON VIII

Triads are built upon each tone of a key.
A triad is named from the scale-degree number of the root; e.g., the following in the key of D-major are the I, V, II, etc.

I V II IV VI III VII

Roman numerals are used as symbols of triads in a key.
The terms tonic, dominant, sub-dominant, etc., are also used; i.e., the tonic triad, the dominant triad, etc.

Drill 15

(1) Write the I, V, II, IV, VI, III and VII triads in each major and minor key.

LESSON IX

It will be found that in each major key
the I, IV and V triads are major,
the II, VI and III triads are minor,
the VII triad is diminished.

Maj. Min. Dim.

In each minor key
the I and IV triads are minor,
the V and VI triads are major,
the VII and II triads are diminished,
the III triad is augmented.

Min. Maj. Dim. Aug.

Drill 16

(1) Learn the tables given above.

LESSON X

A triad is often written as a four-tone chord by duplicating one tone, generally the root, and is named from its root and its quality.

Inversions are named in the same manner.

The following would be the C-major chord and the f-minor chord:

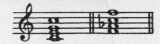

A chord with four different tones, one above the other in 3rds, is a **seventh-chord.**

The added 3rd is the 7th of the chord.

Drill 17

(1) Erect a seventh-chord from each line and space of the staff.

LESSON XI

All seventh-chords are dissonant. The quality of a seventh-chord is determined from the quality of the triad and the size of the interval of the 7th. The most used seventh-chords are the **dominant seventh,** which has a major triad and a minor 7th, the **small seventh,** which has a minor triad and minor 7th, and the **diminished seventh**, which has a diminished triad and a diminished 7th. The other seventh-chords are given in Lesson XX, page 109.

Dom.7   Small 7   Dim.7

Drill 18

(1) Erect a dominant seventh, a small seventh, and a diminished seventh-chord from C, F, D, G, E, A and B.

CHAPTER I

CONNECTION OF TRIADS

Lesson I

Harmony, the grammar of music, is generally presented through the connection of chords for four-part vocal music. The laws and restrictions governing the progressions of four vocal parts give the fundamental technique for the handling of tones in all types of musical composition.

The practical range of each voice part—soprano, alto, tenor and bass—is given below:

    Soprano   Alto   Tenor   Bass

In arranging the tones of a chord, the soprano should not be more than an octave above the alto.

The tenor should not be more than an octave below the alto.

But the bass may be more than an octave from the tenor.

The soprano and alto are written on the treble staff, the tenor and bass on the bass staff. The stems of the notes for the soprano and tenor go up on the right side of the note, for alto and bass down on the left side of the note.

The doubled root, 3rd or 5th of a chord, may be used in the soprano and the chord is said to be in the **position** of the 8ve, 3rd or 5th.

The number given above the soprano indicates the position of the chord. A plus-sign (+) indicates that the soprano is on the higher of the two possible tones within the range; a minus-sign (−) indicates that it is on the lower.

+8 +3 −5 −5 −3 +5 +8 +8 −8 +3

In the first lessons only triads with a doubled root will be used. If the soprano and alto or the tenor and bass sing the same pitch, a unison, one note-head is used with a stem on the right for the upper voice and a stem on the left for the lower voice. When a whole note unison is desired two note-heads are used.

Drill 1

(1) Fill in the alto and tenor voices of the following chords:

If the 3rd or 5th of the chord is in the soprano, place the doubled root before placing the other tone.

If the doubled root is in the given soprano, place the chord 3rd first.

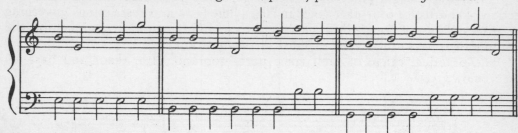

In these and the following four-part harmony exercises, the stems of all the notes for the soprano go up; for the bass, down.

Generally in the writing of a melody, the stems of the notes on the middle line of the staff go up or down as the notes are approached from above or below. For notes above the middle line, the stems go down; below the middle line, the stems go up.

(2) Erect the A, D and F chords in as many ways as possible, using the examples given above as models.

(3) Sing a major chord in arpeggio form from each tone, using the following rhythm in 4-4. Sing the letter-names of the tones or the fixed "do" syllables.

Play the root and think the sound of the chord before singing.

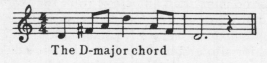

The D-major chord

Lesson II

The **progression** of one chord to another gives an accent and establishes a feeling of tonality, whereas the repetition of a chord, as in Illustration **a,** gives only a feeling of pulse, not progression. When chords change, as in **b,** there is a feeling of progression. In **c,** the progression of the C-major chord to the G-major chord to the C-major chord establishes the Key of C. The progression of the C-major chord to the D-major chord to the G-major chord establishes the Key of G.

The most usual progression of chord-roots is up and down a 5th, as chords are erected upon the tones of the key.   (See page 13.)

A chord may progress to a chord whose root is a 5th below.

In the three upper voices:

>Keep the common tone in the same voice.
>The other tones move up.

The common tone is the tone of the same letter-name found in both chords.

NOTE. In this and the other examples and exercises for the technique of voice-leading, the quality and relation of the chords to the key-center are not considered. This technique is a process applicable to all chords. Each measure is a separate example.

Drill 2

(**1**)   Fill in the alto and tenor voices of the following chords:

(**2**)   Connect the chords of D, F, A and B in all three positions with the chords whose roots are a 5th below.

(**3**)   Sing a minor chord in arpeggio form from each tone—as in Drill 1, No. 3.

Lesson III

A chord may progress to a chord whose root is a 5th above.

In the three upper voices:

>Keep the common tone in the same voice.
>The other voices move down.

Drill 3

(1)   Fill in the alto and tenor voices of the following chords:

(2)   Connect the chords of E, F, G and B in all positions with the chords whose roots are a 5th above.

(3)   Sing chord-roots up and down a perfect 5th from each tone.   Think major chords above each root.   Sing a major chord in arpeggio form from each of these tones.

Lesson IV

Chords are named from the scale-degree number of the root.   In the Key of C the chord built on C is the I chord (one chord), the G-chord is the V chord (five chord), the F-chord is the IV chord (four chord), etc.   (See page 13.)

Roman numerals are used as symbols of chords.

The terms, tonic, dominant, sub-dominant, etc., are also used.

In all keys the tonic or I chord is the key-center and a rest chord.   The root of the I chord may progress to the root of any chord.   All other chords are active and will progress back to the I chord directly or through other chords.

A detailed discussion of the progression of chord-roots is given on page 39.

Since chords are built upon the tones of the key which are related in 5ths, the nearest related chords to the tonic are the dominant, the 5th above, and the sub-dominant, the 5th below.   These are the principal chords in each key.

It is possible to progress from the I to the V chord or from the I to the IV chord.   Both the IV and the V chords will progress back to the I chord.

D	A	D	D	A	D	d	A	d
I	V	I	I	V	I	I	V	I

D G D   D G D   d g d
I IV I   I IV I   I IV I

Drill 4

(1) Fill in the soprano, alto and tenor voices of the following drills in the keys of C-major and c-minor, F-major and f-minor:

An accidental under a bass note is applied to the tone a 3rd above, i.e., in Exercise 5 a B♮.

Under each chord write its letter-name, using a capital letter for major chords, a small letter for minor chords. Under this write the number-name of the chord in Roman numerals.

(2)   Connect the I, V, I and I, IV, I in the keys of D, E, G, A and B, major and minor.

(3)   Sing the following chords in each major and minor key:

I V I IV I V I

I IV I V I IV I

I V I V I IV I

I IV I IV I V I

These chords may be sung in arpeggio form, using the staff letter-names or fixed "do" syllables. The composite sound of each chord should be heard before the arpeggio is sung. The following rhythm in 4-4 is good timing, the second measure giving ample opportunity for thinking and hearing mentally the chord which follows. This work should be done in class, orally, the instructor asking for the chords. The instructor should name the following chord on the third pulse of the second measure. This oral drill should be given first from the letter-name, i.e., C-major, G-major, etc., then from the symbol, i.e., the I chord, the V chord, etc.

(4)   Construct original chord-phrases in duple-meter in each major key, using the I, IV and V chords according to the following instructions:

A **phrase** is the smallest form in music expressing a complete thought. It is generally four measures long and is determined by a stop or a **cadence.**

A chord is used for each pulse of the meter in the first three measures. The last measure will have only the I chord.

The phrase will begin with the I chord.

A chord may be repeated within the measure. When a chord is repeated the position is generally changed.

The chord is changed over the bar.

The chord preceding the tonic at the end is usually the dominant (V chord). This progression V-I at the end of a phrase is an **authentic cadence.** It is a **perfect authentic cadence,** and parallels a period in punctuation, if the I chord is in the position of the octave. This is a complete and final close. It is an **imperfect authentic cadence** if the I chord is in the position of the 3rd or 5th. This gives an incomplete close and parallels a question in punctuation.

It is also possible to precede the final I chord with a IV chord. This progression IV-I at the end of a phrase is known as a **plagal cadence.**

Rule the staff for four measures. Place two dots, representing the metric pulses, under each measure. Write the symbol of the first chord and the cadence chords.

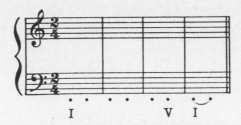

Fill in the other pulses, using the progressions I, IV, I and I, V, I. Chord repetition in at least one measure is recommended because the changing of the position of a chord gives a more interesting melody.

After the chords are determined, write in the bass notes.

Next fill in the first chord using any position, the 8ve, 3rd or 5th, and connect with the following chord according to the rules of voice-leading given in the preceding drill.

In the accompanying exercise the position of the 3rd is used in the first chord. As this chord is repeated in the measure the voices are rearranged with the 5th in the soprano. Next the root progresses down a 5th, the common tone is held and the other voices move up a 2nd. The soprano is D, not from choice, but because of the action of the chord-root. Next the root progresses up a 5th, the common tone is held, the other voices move down. Next the root moves up a 5th (down a 4th), the common tone is held, the other voices move down. The next chord is a repetition. The soprano jumps to another position. Next the root progresses down a 5th (up a 4th), the common tone is held, the other voices move up. The only choice of melody-tones is in the measures where there is chord repetition. The other tones of the melody are the result of the progression of the chord-roots.

The same chord-root and progression is obtained if the bass moves down a 5th or up a 4th; also if it moves up a 5th or down a 4th. The choice of direction in the movement of the bass is determined by the range of the bass and position of the tenor. It is also best to keep contrary motion between the soprano and bass.

(5) Fill in the alto and tenor voices of the following chord-phrases: When possible these and all other exercises should be taken from dictation, the instructor playing all four voices.

NOTE. The following instructions for the dictation of chord drills and exercises may be helpful:
No pedal should be used.
Play at a tempo ranging from MM. 50 to 52.
Play with a firm even touch, giving a little prominence to the outer voices.
Give the tonality and the meter.
First playing, the student listens to the sound without analysing.
Second playing, the student concentrates upon and visualizes the bass. Writes the bass.
Third playing, the student concentrates upon and visualizes the soprano. Writes the soprano.
Fourth playing, the student concentrates upon the quality and writes the letter-name and quality under each chord. Next he writes the symbols.
Added instructions: At first it may be necessary to repeat a playing for the bass or soprano. For violinists and singers it is a good plan to allow the student to hum the bass as it is being played. To make certain that students are visualizing have them indicate the movement of a voice-part on an imaginary staff in the air. In all cases insist that they visualize the tones upon the staff, **not upon the keyboard.**

(6) Add the soprano, alto and tenor voices above the following basses. Each bass tone is the root of a chord. The number above indicates the part of the chord to be used in the soprano; i.e., in bass **a**, the first chord is to be in the position of the 8ve. When no number is given the choice of position is left to the student.

Work in the following manner:

 Establish the tonality with the piano or some other instrument.

 Keeping strict time at a moderately slow tempo, sing the bass until it is firmly fixed in your mind.

 Think the sound, hearing the quality of each chord, and visualizing the notes forming the chord.

After visualizing the indicated soprano of the first chord, hear and visualize the soprano as the chord progresses. The soprano will be determined by the action of the chord-roots; i.e., in bass **a**, when the B♭ is repeated in Measure 1, the soprano may move up to D or down to F. If you have heard it moving up to D, it will progress to E♭ and back to D as the roots progress to E♭ and B♭ in Measure 2. In Measure 3 as the bass moves up a 5th, the soprano will move down to C. The soprano is indicated for the repeated F.

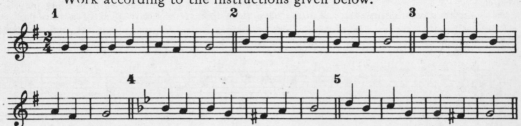

(7) The following melodies are to be harmonized using the progressions I, V, I and I, IV, I:

When a tone is repeated the chord should be changed.

All skips are in the same chord.

Work according to the instructions given below.

First establish the key by singing the progressions I, V, I and I, IV, I in arpeggio form.

Sing the melody several times at a moderate tempo until its sound is thoroughly fixed in the mind. Think the melody, seeing and hearing the chord-roots which will harmonize the soprano. Visualize the bass on the G-staff as a counter-melody.

Sing the bass, hearing the melody mentally.

Sing the bass, playing the melody on some instrument. If this work is done in class, sing the bass and melody as a two-part exercise. In classes of mixed voices first have the girls sing the soprano, boys the bass, then the reverse.

Write the bass.

Fill in the alto and tenor voices.

When possible sing as a four-part exercise.

(8) Analyze the following folk-song:

Moderato

Play several times until the composition can be heard mentally.

Mark each chord with its letter-name and quality. It is most important that this analysis should be done from *what is heard* and not from the notes on the printed page.

Mark each chord with its symbol name.

Mark and name the cadences.

There are tones which are foreign to the chord. These are:

Passing Tones, i.e., tones which move along the scale step-wise or chromatically between chord-tones as the G and B♭ on the up-beat of Measure 1; or—

Neighboring Tones, i.e., tones preceded and followed by the same chord-tone. There are two kinds of neighboring tones, the **upper neighbor,** the tone above a chord-tone, and the **lower neighbor,** the tone below a chord-tone. The lower neighbor is generally one half-step below and the upper neighbor agrees with the scale. The E and G in Measure 8 are lower neighbors. In the key of C, the upper and lower neighbors of E are F and D♯, in the key of E, F♯ and D♯.

NOTE: When possible, this analysis should be done orally.
        Suggestions for the instructor:
          Give the tonality.
          Play the composition once or twice, the class beating time, determining the meter.
          Class determines the cadences.
          Then, working one phrase at a time, class determines:
            The letter-names of the chords.
            The symbol-names of the chords.

LESSON V

A chord may progress to a chord whose root is a 4th above.

The voice-leading may be the same as when the root progresses down a 5th, or—

All three upper voices may move down.

Drill 5

(1)   Fill in the soprano, alto and tenor voices of the following exercises. Each exercise is to be worked in two ways:

    Keeping the common tone, other voices moving up.

    All voices moving down, as illustrated above.

(2) Sing the following chords in the keys of A-major and a-minor, using the meter and rhythm given on page 20.

I IV I V I

I V I IV I V I

(3) Fill in the alto and tenor voices of the following exercises. When possible these exercises should be taken from dictation. Sing the bass of each exercise and hear mentally the soprano and the chord-quality before filling in.

(4) Fill in the alto and tenor voices of the following chord-phrases.

(5) Fill in the soprano, alto and tenor voices of the following basses. Work as instructed on page 22.

When a bass-tone is repeated change the position of the chord.

(6) Harmonize the following melodies, using the I, IV and V chords. Work as instructed on page 23.

In all chord connection try to keep the common tone. When this is not possible because of the movement of the soprano apply the point of the lesson.

(7) Analyze the following folk-song according to instructions given on page 24.

Moderato

Folk-Song

(8)   Construct original chord-phrases in duple and triple meter applying the material of this lesson, following the instructions given on page 20.

Lesson VI

A chord may progress to a chord whose root is a 4th below.
The voice-leading may be:
    The same as when the root progresses up a 5th, or—
    All three upper voices may move up.

Drill 6

(1)   Fill in the soprano, alto and tenor voices of the following exercises.
Each exercise is to be worked in two ways:
    Keeping the common tone, other voices moving down.
    The three upper voices moving up, as illustrated above.

(2)   Sing the following chords in the Keys of G-major and g-minor, using the meter and rhythm given on page 20.

I V I IV I

I IV I IV I V I

(3) Fill in the alto and tenor voices of the following exercises. Sing the bass of each exercise and hear mentally the soprano and the chord-quality before filling in.

(4) Fill in the alto and tenor voices of the following chord-phrases.

(5) Fill in the soprano, alto and tenor voices of the following basses.

NOTE. In bass **b,** the numbers above the first tone indicate the change of position.

(6) Harmonize the following melodies, using the I, IV and V chords.
In all chord connection try to keep the common tone.

When this is not possible because of the movement of the soprano, apply the points of this and the preceding lesson.

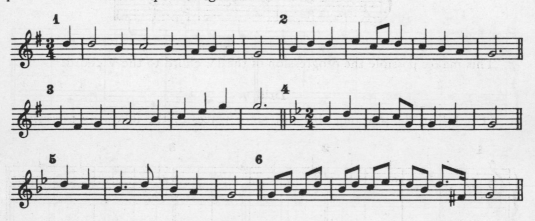

(7) Analyze the following folk-song according to instructions given on page 24.

Moderato

Folk-Song

(8)   Construct original chord-phrases in duple and triple meter, applying the material of this lesson, following the instructions given on page 20.

LESSON VII

A chord may progress to a chord whose root is a 2nd above.
The three upper voices will move down.

This makes possible the progression of the IV chord to the V chord.

Drill 7

(1)   Fill in the soprano, alto and tenor voices of the following exercises:

(2)   Sing the following chords in the key of D-major and d-minor, using the meter and rhythm given on page 20.

I IV I IV V I

I IV V I V I

I V I IV I IV V I

(3)   Fill in the alto and tenor voices of the following exercises.   Sing the bass of each exercise and hear mentally the soprano and the chord-quality before filling in.

(4) Fill in the alto and tenor voices of the following chord-phrases:

(5) Fill in the soprano, alto and tenor voices of the following basses:

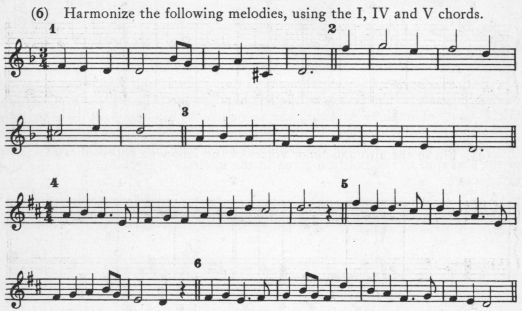

(6)   Harmonize the following melodies, using the I, IV and V chords.

(7)   Analyze the following piano composition according to instructions on page 24.

Allegro   Czerny

(8)   Construct original chord-phrases in duple and triple meter, applying the material of this lesson, following the instructions given on page 20.

(9)   Harmonize the following melodies, using the style of piano accompaniment given in the model.

When the harmonic material presented in these lessons is used in writing for the piano or other instruments, the same fundamental laws as in four-part vocal writing govern the action of the tones. The manner of arranging these tones is peculiar to the instrument.

In writing for the piano strict four-part vocal style is seldom used for any length of time. The chords may be broken in arpeggio form, étude style, or used in some characteristic style of accompaniment. The adopted style of accompaniment is used throughout a short composition, and in longer compositions for at least an entire section.

There are fewer chord changes in a phrase of piano music than in a four-part harmony exercise, as the recurrence of the accompanying rhythmic figure will mark the pulse. It is possible to use one chord for two measures.

With this style of accompaniment in duple meter only one chord is possible in each measure. The octave in the left hand at the beginning of each measure is the bass. The three tones on the second pulse are the body of the chord. These tones can be arranged in any of the following ways, depending upon the range of the melody. These voices should never go below C on the second space of the bass staff. The position given in the model will be found to be the most satisfactory.

The choice of bass is determined as in four-part writing except that there will be but one chord to a measure. In the model the consecutive skips in Measure 1 demand the D-chord; the wide skip in Measure 2 the G-chord; the wide skip in Measure 3 the A-chord. For the melodic progression B to A the root of the G-chord could have progressed up a 5th to the D-chord but this would not have accommodated the wide skip from A to C#, or given the progression of the V to the I chord for the cadence.

The group of tones in the left hand on the second pulse should remain in the same register, and is subject to the rules of four-part writing; e.g., the common tone is held, the other voices moving diatonically up or down, etc.

Lesson VIII

A chord may progress to a chord whose root is a 2nd below.
The three upper voices will move up.

This makes possible the progression of the V chord to the IV chord. The IV chord will generally return to the V chord, or it may progress to the I chord.

Drill 8

(1) Fill in the soprano, alto and tenor voices of the following exercises:

(2) Sing the following chords in the key of E-flat major and e-flat minor, using the meter and rhythm given on page 20.

I V I IV V IV V I

I IV V IV V I

I IV I V IV V I

(3) Fill in the alto and tenor voices of the following exercises. Sing the bass of each exercise and hear mentally the soprano and the chord-quality before filling in.

Note that the progression of the V chord to the IV is generally used to delay the resolution of the V chord.

(4) Fill in the alto and tenor voices of the following chord-phrases. These phrases should be taken from dictation when possible.

(5)   Fill in the soprano, alto and tenor voices of the following basses.   Work as outlined on page 22.

(6)   Harmonize the following melodies, using the I, IV and V chords.

(7)   Analyze the following piano composition according to instructions given on page 24.

Czerny

(8) Construct original chord-phrases in duple and triple meter, applying the material of this lesson, following the instructions on page 20. Use the exercises of (4) as a model.

(9) Harmonize the following melodies, using the style of piano accompaniment given in the model. Work according to instructions given on page 32.

NOTE. In Melody 6 do not harmonize the up-beat.

Moderato

(**10**)   Develop the following measure into a phrase of piano music.

This measure is a **motive**.   The rhythm and the direction of the movement of the tones are characteristic of the motive.

A motive may be used in the following ways:

In exact repetition

In modified repetition

In exact sequence

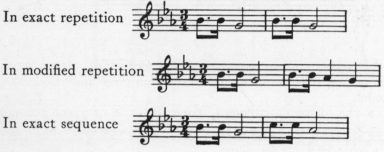

In modified sequence

by changing size of interval

by adding tones

by inversion

The motive may recur in Measure 2 as in Melodies 2, 3 and 5 of Section 9. When the motive is used in Measure 2 it is usual to have new material in Measure 3.

New material may be used in Measure 2 as in Melodies 1 and 4.   With this use it is best to have the motive again in Measure 3.

Plan and write the bass first, making either an authentic or a plagal cadence.

Then develop the melody from the motive using the melodies of Section 9 as models.

The rhythms used in a melody are quite as important as the pitches.

The measure in which the motive is used will retain the rhythm of the motive in exact or slightly modified form.   In the other measures it is generally necessary to have a new rhythmic arrangement which is a logical development and balance to the rhythm of the motive.

The following suggestions may be helpful in developing the rhythms:

Beating time, intone a pitch for each pulse of the meter in the phrase.

After repeating this several times, intone the rhythm of the given motive for the first two measures, allowing the momentum to suggest what is to be used in Measure 3. After this third measure is determined and written down, experiment with other combinations. In the same way use the figure in Measures 1 and 3, inventing new material for Measure 2.

(11) Invent and develop original motives, using the style of accompaniment given above.

LESSON IX

A chord may progress to a chord whose root is a 3rd below.

Keep the common tones.
The other voice moves up.

Drill 9

(1) Fill in the soprano, alto and tenor voices of the following exercises:

The progression of chord-roots down in 3rds produces the I, VI, IV, II, VII, V, III, I chords thus adding four new chords, the VI, II, VII and III.

The roots of these chords may progress up and down a 5th, 4th and 2nd the same as the roots of the I, IV and V chords.

The VII chord is seldom used as a fundamental chord. The method of handling the VII chord is given in Lesson XV.

Certain chord-progressions are obviously more satisfying than others. This is due to the following facts:

Chords are built upon the tones of the key. (See Chapter I of the Introduction.) These tones are related in 5ths, starting with the key-tone which is the key-center and at rest.

The other tones are active, and their activity varies in intensity according to their proximity to the key-center.

It is a law of gravity that falling particles increase in activity until they come to rest.   Therefore, as soon as any one of these active chords is used, it will progress to a more active chord until it comes to rest upon the I chord, the key-center.

The progression of an active chord to one more active is **normal** or **regular progression.**

It is possible to take an active chord to a chord which is less active.   This is **irregular** or **regressive movement,** and is generally only the postponing of normal progression, and is used for that purpose.

It is obvious that progressions may be made out from the key-center, the I chord.

The regular or normal progression of chord-roots down in 5ths (harmonic progression) gives the

VII III VI II V I

Because of its diminished quality, derivation and sound, the VII chord (treated in Lesson XV) is not often used in fundamental form or in this relation.

The normal progression of chord-roots down in 3rds, gives the

I VI IV II VII V III I

The note about the VII chord given above applies in these progressions.

Also, the progression of the II chord directly to the V chord is almost imperative because of the harmonic activity and proximity of its root to the key-center.

II V I

The III chord is sometimes used in this way, but because of the activity of the V chord it is difficult to hear the movement of the V chord to the III chord as a progression.   It sounds as if the root of the III chord is an anticipation of the 3rd of the I chord which follows.

II   V   III   I

The normal progression of chord-roots up a 3rd is the III chord to the V chord.

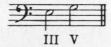

III V

The normal progressions of chord-roots up a 2nd are the III chord to the IV chord and the IV chord to the V chord.

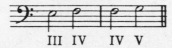

III IV   IV V

The normal progressions of chord-roots down a 2nd are the VI chord to the V chord, the III chord to the II chord and the II chord to the I chord.

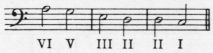

VI V   III II   II I

The **irregular or regressive movement of chord-roots** is up in 5ths or down in 4ths

(VII)
III
VI
II
V
I
IV

V   II   VI   III VII

The VII chord is seldom used in this series.

The **irregular or regressive movement of chord-roots in 3rds** is up from the II, IV, V and VI chords.

II   IV   IV   VI   V   VII   VI   I

The **regressive movement of chord-roots up a 2nd** is from the II and V chords.

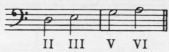

II III   V   VI

The **regressive movement of chord-roots down a 2nd** is from the V and the IV chords.

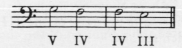

V   IV   IV   III

The choice of root-progressions depends entirely upon what is to be expressed, and the form through which the expression is made. Therein lies the genius of the composer. The facts given above may enable the student better to understand the purpose of the exercises in these lessons, and add to his appreciation of the music which he studies. This material will be mastered as the exercises of the succeeding lessons are worked.

(2)   Sing the following chords in the key of A♭-major, using the meter and rhythm given on page 20.

Review the lesson on the quality of triads on page 13 (Lesson IX) of the introduction.

I VI IV II V I

I VI II V VI IV V I

I IV V VI IV II V I

In a♭-minor:

I VI IV V VI V I

I V VI IV V I

I VI V IV VI V I

(3)   Fill in the alto and tenor voices of the following exercises. Thinking from the bass, hear each chord mentally while writing.

(4)   Fill in the alto and tenor voices of the following chord-phrases:

In harmonizing a repeated tone, the root of the chord may move down a 3rd.

In minor, when the VI chord progresses down to the V chord, or the V chord up to the VI chord, double the 3rd in the VI chord. This avoids the unmelodic progression of an augmented 2nd between the 6th and 7th degrees.

(5) Fill in the soprano, alto and tenor voices of the following basses. Sing each chord in arpeggio form as in Section 2.

(6) Harmonize the following melodies, using the chords of this lesson.

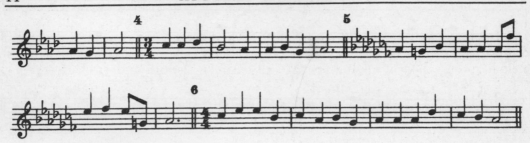

(7) Analyze the following piano arrangement according to instructions given on page 24.

Moderato

Carey

(8) Construct original chord-phrases in duple and triple meter, applying the material of this lesson, following the instructions given on page 20. Use the exercises of Section (4) as models.

(9) Harmonize the following melodies, using the style of piano accompaniment given in the model.

Andante

(10) Develop the following measure into a phrase of piano music, according to instructions given on page 38.

(11) Invent and develop original motives, using the style of accompaniment given above.

LESSON X

A chord may progress to a chord whose root is a 3rd above.

Keep the common tones.
The other voice moves down.

Drill 10

(1) Fill in the soprano, alto and tenor voices of the following exercises:

The most common use of this progression is from the I chord to the III chord, which in turn progresses to the IV chord and harmonizes the melodic progression 8–7–6. (See page 41.)

The voice-leading is normal if the I chord is in **close position, i.e.,** the tenor is not more than an 8ve below the soprano.

I　　III　　IV　　V

But when the I chord is in **open position,** i.e., the tenor more than **an 8ve** from the soprano, it is generally necessary to double the 3rd of the III chord so as to bring the voices of the IV chord, which follows, into position to progress correctly to the V chord.　In effect, the III chord is a passing chord between **the I** and the IV chords.

I　　III　　IV　　V

Another common use of this progression is down a 3rd from any chord and back.

A chord-root may also progress up a 3rd from any chord and back.

In both progressions the chord in the middle is an embellishment of the first chord.

(2)　Sing the following chords in the key of E-major, using the meter and rhythm given on page 20.

I III IV II V I

I VI IV V VI IV VI V I

I III IV II IV V I

In e-minor:

I VI I VI IV V I

I V VI IV VI V I

I IV· V VI I VI V I

(3)   Fill in the alto and tenor voices of the following exercises.   After establishing the tonality with the piano or some other instrument, hear each chord mentally while writing.

In minor, when the progression I, III, IV is used, the descending form of the melodic minor scale is employed for the 7th and 6th degrees.   This changes the quality of the III chord from an augmented chord to a major chord.

(4)   Fill in the alto and tenor voices of the following periods.

A **period** consists of two phrases, the antecedent phrase ending with a cadence upon the dominant, called a **semi-cadence,** and the consequent phrase ending with a perfect authentic cadence.

(5) Fill in the soprano, alto and tenor voices of the following basses. Follow the instructions given on page 22.

(6) Harmonize the following melodies.

In harmonizing a repeated tone the root of a chord may move up or down a 3rd.

Note that in Melody 3 there is a break after the semi-cadence, therefore the rules of voice-leading are ignored.

(7) Analyze the following piano composition, according to instructions given on page 24.

Alla marcia

Folk-Song

(8) Construct original chord-periods in duple and triple meter, applying the material of this lesson. Use the exercises of Section (4) as a model.

In planning the bass for the antecedent phrase aim for a cadence on the dominant, preceded in the third measure by any tone but the tonic. When the tonic is used in the third measure it is apt to give the effect of a cadence in that measure and to destroy the unity of the phrase.

(9) Harmonize the following melodies, using the style of accompaniment given in the model.

(10) Develop the following measure into a parallel period of piano music, using Section (9) as a model.

A period is in **parallel construction** when at least the first measure of the antecedent and the first measure of the consequent phrases are alike.

(11) Invent original motives and develop them into parallel periods, using the style of accompaniment given above.

Drill 11

Review of the First Ten Lessons

(1) Sing the following chords in the key of B♭-major, using the meter and rhythm given on page 20.

I IV II V VI IV V I

I II IV II V VI IV V I

I V VI II IV II V I

In b♭-minor:

I III IV V VI IV V I

I V IV V VI V I

I V III V IV I

(2) Fill in the alto and tenor voices of the following exercises:

(3)   Fill in the alto and tenor voices of the following periods:

(4)   Fill in the soprano, alto and tenor voices of the following basses:

(5) Harmonize the following melodies:

(6) Analyze the following piano composition:

Allegro, deciso molto

Schumann

(7) Construct original chord-periods in duple and triple meter.

(8) Harmonize the following melodies, using the style of accompaniment given in the model.

With this style of accompaniment there may be one or two chords in a measure.

With each change of chord it is necessary to use a new bass tone. (See the second phrase of the model.)

In these melodies passing-tones are used on the subdivisions of the pulses to fill in the skips between chord-tones.

Chord-tones are used on the pulses.

All skips are from chord-tones.

Note the use of passing tones in these melodies.

Moderato

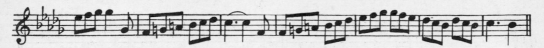

(9) Develop the following measure into a parallel period of piano music.

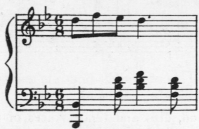

(10) Invent original motives and develop them into parallel periods using the style of accompaniment given above.

LESSON XI

EXCEPTIONAL VOICE-LEADING

The progressions given in Lessons XI and XII will be found in the chorales of Bach. These progressions are exceptional, and should not be used until it has been proven that the normal voice-leading given in the preceding lessons is not possible. The progressions in Lesson XI are more commonly used than those in Lesson XII.

When the root of a chord moves up a 2nd or up a 4th.

All three upper voices may move down as in Lesson V, page 24 and Lesson VII, page 30. Or—

One voice may move up a 2nd, doubling the 3rd in the chord of resolution.

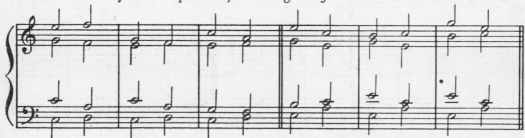

A doubled 3rd is always possible in the II, VI, III and VII chords.

A doubled 3rd rarely occurs in the I, IV and V chords.

The above progressions are used when progressing to the II, VI or III chord.

In progressing from a chord with a doubled 3rd, **the doubled tone moves in contrary motion.**

If the doubled tone is a common tone, hold one tone stationary, preferably the tone in the inner voice.

Drill 12

(1) Fill in the soprano, alto and tenor voices of the following exercises, each in two ways:

       First, according to Lessons V and VII.

       Then, according to examples given above.

NOTE—Double the 3rd of the first chord of exercises 4, 5, 6, 7, 8, 9, 10.

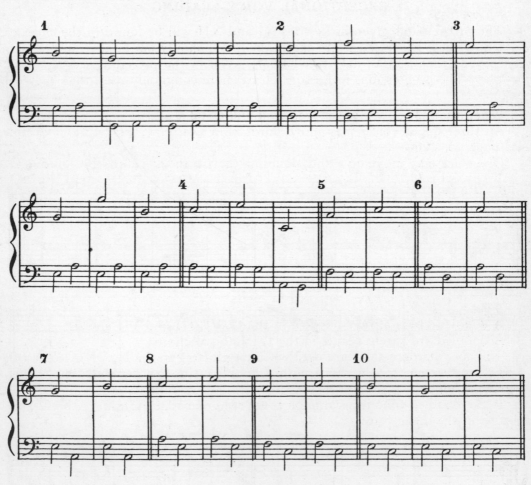

(2) Fill in the alto and tenor voices of the following exercises.

Establish the tonality upon some instrument before writing.

These exercises should be played upon the piano many times, so that the ear may become familiar with the sound of these progressions.

(3) Fill in the alto and tenor voices of the following periods:

(4)   Fill in the soprano, alto and tenor voices of the following basses, according to instructions given on page 22.

(5)   Harmonize the following melodies according to instructions given on page 23.

(6)   Analyze the following piano composition:

Adagio

Folk-Song

(7) Construct original chord periods in duple and triple meter, using the exercises in Section (3) as models.

(8) Harmonize the following melodies, using the style of accompaniment given in the model.

Andante

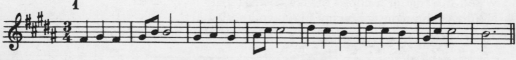

1

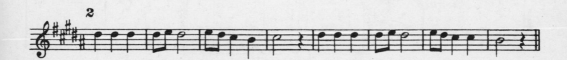

2

(9) Develop the following measure into a contrasting period of piano music, using Section (8) as a model.

A period is in **contrasting construction** when the first measure of the consequent phrase is different from the first measure of the antecedent phrase.

Andante

(10) Invent original motives and develop them into contrasting periods, using the style of accompaniment given above.

LESSON XII

The progressions given in this lesson are principally for reference. It is not essential at this stage of development that this lesson be mastered.

When a root of a chord moves down a 5th:
The 3rd of the chord may move up a 4th.

When the root of a chord moves down a 3rd:
Hold the common tones;
The other voice jumps, doubling the 3rd of the chord resolution.

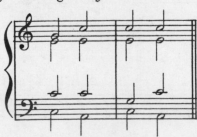

When the root of a chord moves up a 3rd:
One voice may move up, doubling the 3rd of the chord of resolution.

When the root of a chord progresses up a 4th or a 5th from a chord with a doubled 3rd:
Each note of the doubled tone may move down, one diatonically or with a narrow skip, the other with a wide skip.

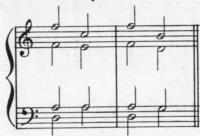

When the root of a chord progresses down a 3rd from a chord with a doubled 3rd:
Keep the common tone;
The other voices move up a 4th.

Drill 13

(1) Fill in the soprano, alto and tenor voices of the following exercises, each in two ways:

First, according to Lessons II to X.
Then, according to examples given above.

(2)   Fill in the alto and tenor voices of the following exercises:

(3)   Fill in the alto and tenor voices of the following exercises:

Note. The exercises in this lesson are parts of chorales.   Many of the harmonizations are by Bach.

(4)   Fill in the soprano, alto and tenor voices of the following basses, according to the instructions given on page 22.

(5)   Harmonize the following melodies according to the instructions given on page 23.

(6) Analyze the following piano composition:

Andante

Methfessel

(7) Construct original chorales in duple meter, using the exercises in Sections (3) and (5) as models.

(8) Harmonize the following melodies, using the style of accompaniment given in the model.

(9) Develop the following measure into a contrasting period for piano, using Section (8) as a model. Use neighboring tones and passing tones.

Allegretto

(10) Invent original motives and develop them into contrasting periods, using the style of accompaniment given above.

DOUBLING

The doubled root of all chords is desirable, since it gives sonority and emphasizes the individual quality of the chord.

In the I, IV and V chords a doubled 5th is possible; in the VI, II and III chords a doubled 3rd is possible.

The doubling of any part of a chord other than the root will vary the quality of the chord. The doubled 5th in the I, IV and V chords upsets the balance of the chord and causes the mind to move down from the chord 5th to the root, instead of up from the root. The doubled 3rd in these chords is muddy and to some ears discordant. The doubled 3rd in the VI, II and III chords tends to make them take on the quality of the I, IV and V chords. A doubled 5th in these chords is unpleasant and harsh.

From the above it will be found that, when doubling a tone other than the root of the chord, the doubled 1st, 4th and 5th degrees of the scale are the most satisfactory to the ear.

When a tone is sounded, the overtones which give quality to the tone are set in vibration, the consonant overtones, the 8ve, 3rd and 5th being most prominent.

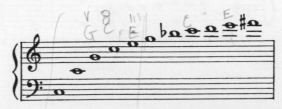

A tone which is doubled will be more prominent, and therefore its overtones will also be more prominent. The consonant overtones of the 1st, 4th and 5th degrees of the scale are all a part of the key. The consonant overtones of the 2nd, 3rd, 6th and 7th degrees have one or more tones foreign to the tones of the key.

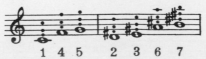

1 4 5   2 3 6 7

This accounts for the unsatisfactory and, to some ears, discordant sound of the following chords:

In a major key, a doubled third in the minor chords, the II, VI and III, tends to make them less characteristically minor in quality and therefore more in keeping with the major tonality.

It is possible to have irregular doubling in any chord if it is caused by the diatonic leading of voice-parts. As four-part harmony is in reality four-voice counterpoint, the ear hears each voice-part as a contrapuntal line, and in following these lines will accept an irregular doubling, especially if it occurs on an unaccented pulse.

Bach

CHAPTER II

INVERSIONS OF TRIADS

Lesson XIII

A chord is in the **first inversion** when the 3rd of the chord is in the bass.

The doubling is the same as when the root is in the bass. The chord 5th may also be doubled.

The figured bass symbol for a first inversion is a 6 written below the bass note.

Drill 14

(1) Fill in the alto and tenor voices of the following chords:

A chord may be followed by its first inversion and a first inversion may be followed by its fundamental chord.

The root and the 3rd of the chord may interchange.

The other voices remain stationary.

One or two voices may move in parallel direction to the bass.

One or two voices may move in opposite direction to the bass.

The choice of one of these possibilities is governed by the smoothness with which the voices of the second chord will lead into the following chord.

(2) Fill in the soprano, alto and tenor voices of the following exercise:

A fundamental chord may progress to a first inversion whose bass has the same tone or a tone any interval above or below.

The bass of a chord in the first inversion may progress to a fundamental chord whose root has the same tone or a tone any interval above or below.

The doubled tone moves in contrary motion.

When the doubled tone is a common tone one tone is held, the other generally moves in contrary motion to the bass. If the common tone is in both the tenor and the soprano, the soprano generally moves.

It is not usual for the bass to jump more than a 3rd to or from a first inversion except when approaching the II chord in its first inversion at the cadence. See Lesson XIV, page 75.

(3)   Fill in the soprano, alto and tenor voices of the following exercises:

(4)   Fill in the alto and tenor voices of the following exercises:

In taking these exercises from dictation, work in the usual way, writing first the bass, then the soprano.

A first inversion may be determined in several ways. It is weaker in sound than the fundamental chord and sounds top-heavy, particularly when the root is in the soprano. When it is preceded or followed by the same fundamental chord it is recognized as a rearrangement of the chord.

The surest way to determine first inversions is to analyze the quality from each bass tone. In major, if the 1st, 4th or 5th degrees of the scale are in the bass a major chord is expected; if the 2nd, 3rd or 6th degrees a minor chord; if the 7th degree a diminished chord. First inversions on these bass tones have the opposite quality; i.e., if a minor chord is heard with the 1st, 4th or 5th degrees in the bass it is a first inversion, if a major chord is heard with the 3rd, 6th or 7th degrees in the bass it is a first inversion.

In symbolizing a first inversion either a $_6$ or a $_1$ may be placed on the lower right-hand side of the letter and number name; e.g., the C chord in the first inversion is written C_1 or C_6, and in the key of C, I_1 or I_6.

(5) Fill in the alto and tenor voices of the following periods:

(6)   Fill in the soprano, alto and tenor voices of the following basses:

In working figured basses, if the first inversion of the I, IV or V chord is given, it is best, when possible, to have the root in the soprano. First inversions of the II, III and VI chords may have the 3rd or root in the soprano.

Sing the chords indicated in the following basses using the meter and rhythms given on page 20.

(7)   Harmonize the following melodies:

In harmonizing melodies using inversions sing the melody through several times until the sound is firmly established in the mind.

Sing the first phrase hearing the fundamental chord qualities; i.e., the E-major chord, the A-major chord, etc.

In Melody No. 1, Measure 1, the chords are E-major and A-major; Measure 2, B-major and E-major.

Next sing the phrase visualizing the bass, using fundamental chords only.

Sing the phrase again visualizing the bass using first inversions wherever possible.

In Melody 1, Measure 1, the bass could be E, G♯ leading into A. When the C♯ in the melody moves down to A, the A in the bass could move up to C♯.

In Measure 2 a D♯ could be used in the bass for the repeated B.

A first inversion may be used:

> to harmonize a repeated tone;
> to harmonize skips in the same chord; and,
> in the middle of the phrase, in place of a fundamental chord to prevent a cadential effect.   (See Sec. 5, Ex. 1, Measure 2.)

(8) Analyze the following folk-song:

A phrase may be extended at the end by repeating the cadence in exact form or with melodic modifications.

The cadence is made in the usual manner except that the I chord may be in the position of the 3rd or 5th, or the I chord in the first inversion may be substituted for the fundamental chord. The rhythm generally continues through the cadence measure forming a bridge to the melody of the measures which form the extension.

In performing a composition with an extension at the end, the extensions must be played in tempo and as a part of the composition so as to carry the attention of the listener past the expected stop in the cadence measure.

(9) Construct original chord-periods in duple and triple meter, using first inversions whenever possible.

(10) Harmonize the following melodies using the style of accompaniment given in the model:

A chord may change without giving a feeling of progression. On the third pulse of Measure 1 of the model the chord changes to B_6, returning to e-minor in Measure 2. In sound, these two measures are the e-minor chord. The B_6 chord is an embellishing chord and is used to enforce the accent in Measure 2. In Measure 3 there is a harmonic progression to the a-minor chord changing on the third pulse to the $f\#_6$ chord. The F# in this chord sounds like an anticipation of

the F♯ in the B-major chord which follows; in Measure 4 there is a progression
to the B-major chord.

(11) Develop the following measure into a period, extended by repetition of the cadence chords using Sections (8) and (10) and models:

Andante

(12) Invent original motives and develop them into periods extended by repetition of the cadence chords, using the style of accompaniment given above.

Lesson XIV

The cadence formula II_1 V I is so important that it justifies a special drill. The II_1 chord is used in place of the IV chord or the fundamental II chord.

Drill 15

(1) Fill in the soprano, alto and tenor voices of the following chords:

(2) Sing the following chords in the key of A♭-major using the meter and rhythms given on page 20:

$$I \quad I_1 \quad IV \quad II \quad II_1 \quad V \quad I$$

$$I \quad II_1 \quad V \quad VI \quad IV \quad II_1 \quad V \quad I$$

$$I \quad II \quad II_1 \quad V \quad I_1 \quad IV \quad II_1 \quad V \quad I$$

(3) Fill in the alto and tenor voices of the following exercises:

(4) Fill in the alto and tenor voices of the following periods. These exercises should be taken from dictation when possible.

(5)   Fill in the soprano, alto and tenor voices of the following basses: Work according to the directions on pages 22 and 43.

(6)   Harmonize the following melodies: Work as directed in Section (7) of the preceding lesson.

(7) Analyze the following piano composition:

A phrase may be extended at the beginning with the rhythmic figure of the accompaniment used as an introduction.

(8) Construct original chord periods in duple and triple meter using the cadence formula given in the drill.

(9) Harmonize the following melodies using the style of accompaniment given in the model:

Extend each of these melodies with an introduction.

Passing tones and neighboring tones may be used on the pulses in place of chord tones. These are **accented passing tones** and **accented neighboring tones**. (See Measures 2, 3, 4, 6, 7, 8 and 10 of the model.)

Folk-Song

(**10**)   Develop the following motive into a period extended at the beginning by an introduction, using Section (9) as a model.

Allegretto

(**11**)   Invent original motives and develop them into periods extended by an introduction, using the style of accompaniment given above.

Lesson XV

The triad on the leading-tone, the VII chord, is generally used in the first inversion, never in the second inversion and rarely, except in sequential progressions, as a fundamental chord.

The 3rd or the 5th of the chord may be doubled, never the root.

It is most used in the first inversion in place of the V chord to harmonize the ascending leading-tone. It may be used to form the Perfect Authentic

Cadence, as the bass and soprano form an authentic cadence in two-voice counterpoint.

$$6 \qquad 6 \qquad 6$$
$$b4 \qquad C \qquad b4 \qquad C \qquad b4 \qquad C$$
$$VII_1 \qquad I \qquad VII_1 \qquad I \qquad VII_1 \qquad I$$

Drill 16

(1) Fill in the alto and tenor voices of the following exercises.

In Exercise 6 the line through the figured bass symbol designates that that tone is raised, i.e., A#.

(2) Sing the following chords in the key of B-major, using the meter and rhythms given on page 20:

I IV II VII₁ I   III   IV VII₁ I

I V I₁ IV   II VII₁ I

In b-minor:

I I₁ IV VII₁ I

I II₁ V VI   IV VII₁ I

(3) Fill in the alto and tenor voices of the following periods: Work according to the directions given on page 71.

In Exercise 3 Measure 7 the dash after the ♯ designates that the same tone is raised in the following chord.

(4) Fill in the soprano, alto and tenor voices of the following basses: Work according to the directions on pages 22 and 43.

(5) Harmonize the following melodies: Work as directed in Section (7) of Drill 14.

(6) Analyze the following piano compositions:

A phrase may be extended at the end by evading the resolution of the V chord, taking its root up or down a 2nd to a fundamental chord, or down a 3rd to a first inversion.

(7) Construct original periods in duple and triple meter using Section (3) as a model.

(8) Harmonize the following melodies using the style of accompaniment given in the model:

(9) Develop the following motive into a period extended at the end by the evasion of the cadence: Use Sections (6) and (8) as models.

(10) Invent original motives and develop them into periods extended by the evasion of the cadence, using the style of accompaniment given above.

Lesson XVI

The bass of a first inversion may move up or down a 2nd or a 3rd to another first inversion.

One voice, generally the soprano, moves in parallel 6ths with the bass.

Another voice moves in parallel 3rds with the bass.

The remaining voice jumps, doubling, alternately, the root and 5th of the chords if they are in duple meter and in sequential groups of two; the root, 3rd and 5th if they are in triple meter and in sequential groups of three.

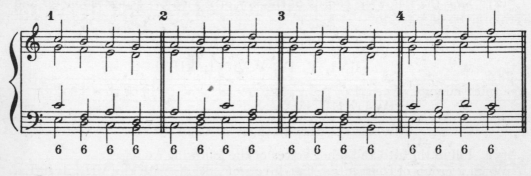

Drill 17

(1) Fill in the soprano, alto and tenor voices of the following exercises:

(2) Sing the following chords in the key of E♭-major, using the meter and rhythm given on page 20.

$$\text{I VI IV}_1 \text{ III}_1 \text{ II}_1 \text{ V I}$$

$$\text{I VI}_1 \text{ V}_1 \text{ IV}_1 \text{ V V}_1 \text{ VI}_1 \text{ VII}_1 \text{ I}$$

In e♭-minor:

$$\text{I IV II}_1 \text{ III}_1 \text{ IV}_1 \text{ V I}$$

$$\text{I V VI IV}_1 \text{ III}_1 \text{ II}_1 \text{ I}_1 \text{ V I}$$

(3) Fill in the alto and tenor voices of the following exercises:

When a group of consecutive first inversions begins with the VII$_1$, as in Ex. 3, it is best to begin with the doubled 3rd.

Consecutive first inversions give the effect of passing-tones in parallel motion, the mind determining the individual quality of only the first and the last chords.

(4) Fill in the alto and tenor voices of the following periods: Write from dictation according to the instructions given on page 71.

In determining what is to be doubled in the first chord of a series of first inversions, the quality of the first and last chords must be considered. Also the voice-leading from the preceding chord into the first chord of the series and from the last chord of the series into the succeeding chord. For example, in Exercise 1 the group begins with the $E\flat_6$-chord (I_1), and ends with the $A\flat_6$-chord (IV_1). In both of these chords the root or the 5th could be doubled. The second chord is the VII_1 chord, in which it is better to double the 5th. In Exercise 4, the first of the group is a VII_1 chord. It is necessary to have a doubled 3rd or 5th.

(5) Fill in the soprano, alto and tenor voices of the following basses:

It is best to have the roots of the chords in the soprano in consecutive inversions.

In Exercise **d,** Measure 6, the figuration 5 6 indicates that the triad is to be used on the first pulse followed by a first inversion on the second pulse.

(6) Harmonize the following melodies:

Consecutive first inversions may be used to harmonize ascending and descending scale-lines and sequential skips of a 3rd.

(7)   Analyze the following composition:

A phrase may be extended by expanding the harmony. A phrase in duple meter, using the chords I V|V.I IV|II V|I|!, could be extended by expanding the last chord into two full measures and the two preceding chords each into one full measure. I V|VI IV|II -|V -|I -|- {||. This expansion gives the feeling of a retard.

Haydn

(8) Construct original periods in duple and triple meter using Section (4) as a model.

(9) Harmonize the following melodies, using the style of accompaniment given in the model.

In progressing from one chord to another, any tone of the first chord which is not common to the second chord may be held over and not allowed to progress until a pulse or a half-pulse later. This tone is called a **suspension.** (See Measure 3.) Suspensions may be tied or re-struck. The voice-leading is normal except that the progression of one tone is retarded. In four-part writing, suspensions may be used in any voice and from any pulse.

NOTE. The accented passing-tones in Measures 2 and 3 of the model are the same in sound as the suspension in Measure 3. The accented passing tones are not a part of the preceding chord.

Folk-Song 4

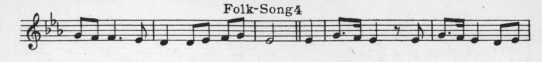

(10) Develop the following motive into a period extended by expansion:

Andantino

(11) Invent original motives and develop them into periods extended by expansion.

LESSON XVII

A chord is in the **second inversion** when its 5th is in the bass.

$$\frac{6}{4}$$

The bass (the 5th of the chord) is doubled.

The figured bass symbol for a second inversion is $\frac{6}{4}$.

The letter and numeral name may be figured

$$C_{\frac{6}{4}} \text{ or } C_2$$

and in the key:

$$I_{\frac{6}{4}} \text{ or } I_2$$

Drill 18

(1) Fill in the alto and tenor voices of the following chords:

The bass of a second inversion may remain stationary resolving to the triad on the same bass tone.

The common tone is held.

The other voices move down.

In this resolution the triad is often figured $\frac{5}{3}$. One bass tone may be used with the figures $\frac{6}{4}\frac{5}{3}$.

(2) Fill in the soprano, alto and tenor voices of the following exercises:

The second inversion resolving in this way is generally used on the accented pulse of the measure. It may be preceded by a fundamental chord or a first inversion on any but the same tone or the bass tone a 3rd above.

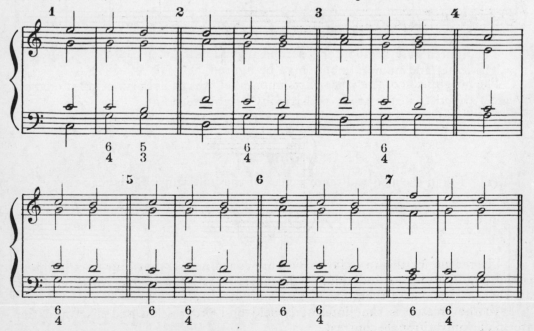

NOTE. All positions of these chords are possible.

The fundamental chord a 3rd below is seldom used.

The tonic six-four (I_2) is the most used second inversion and may form a part of the semi-cadence or the authentic cadence.

(3)   Sing the following chords in F#-major, using the meter and rhythm given on page 20:

I VI IV II_1 I_2 V I

I IV V I_1 II_1 I_2 V I

In f#-minor:

I V VI IV_1 I_2 V I

I IV II_1 V I_1 IV I_2 V I

(4)   Fill in the alto and tenor voices of the following exercises:

The second inversion is not a chord in use or sound. It gives the effect of either passing tones or suspensions from the chord preceding to the chord to which it resolves, and therefore sounds like an embellishment of the latter.

The progression of the voice-parts in parallel 5ths or 8ves is not countenanced by most theorists in the study of harmony or counterpoint.

The reason for this in so far as 8ves are concerned, is that four-part harmony is the handling of four-individual voice-parts. As soon as one voice reinforces another in 8ves one of them has lost its individuality.

Another reason is that interest is held and progression and discrimination are made only through contrast.

Parallel 3rds and 6ths continually vary in quality from major to minor, while in the major mode parallel 5ths are all of the same quality except the diminished 5th from the 7th to the 4th degree of the scale.

It is always allowable to have a diminished 5th follow a perfect 5th.

For the same reason some theorists allow the progression from a diminished 5th to a perfect 5th. This is commonly done by Bach if one of the chords is an inversion.

Consecutive parallel 4ths between the bass and soprano are not used, for the same reason. They are possible between the inner voices because of the constantly changing interval quality between these tones and the bass.

Consecutive parallel 8ves and 5ths will be found in the instrumental and even the vocal music of many composers, but these progressions are obviously used for a special emotional or atmospheric effect.

In strict four-part harmony there are a few progressions where consecutive perfect 5ths between inner voices are possible, because of the unessential quality of one of the chords.

For example, the following voice-leading is correct because of the unessential quality of the $\frac{6}{4}$ chord.

Up to this point consecutive 5ths and 8ves have not been possible if the suggestions for voice-leading have been followed.

(5) Fill in the alto and tenor voices of the following periods:

In triple meter the $\frac{6}{4}$ chord may be used upon the second pulse of the next to the last measure. (See No. 3.)

(6)   Fill in the soprano, alto and tenor voices of the following basses:

(7)   Harmonize the following melodies:

The I_2 V is used to harmonize the melodic progressions 1–7, 3–2, 5–5 at the semi-cadence and 3–2, 1–7 at the final cadence.

(8) Analyze the following piano arrangement:

A double period is generally sixteen measures in length with a semi-cadence in the eighth measure. In the fourth measure there is a light cadence upon the I chord in the position of the 3rd or 5th, or upon the I_6 chord. This causes a break and a feeling of suspension in the thought, and makes the following four measures a continuation and completion of the thought of the antecedent phrase.

The remaining eight measures form a consequent phrase.

There is a light cadence in the twelfth measure which may be the same cadence as in the fourth measure; or may be made upon the IV chord; or may in any way evade the authentic cadence.

The last four measures complete the thought.

Haydn

(9) Construct original periods in duple and triple meter using Section (5) as a model.

(10) Harmonize the following melodies, using the style of accompaniment given in the model:

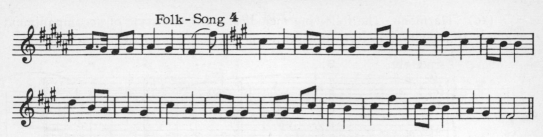

Folk-Song 4

(11) Develop the following motive into a double period.

Andante

dolce

(12) Invent original motives and develop them into double periods.

Lesson XVIII

The second inversion of a chord on an unaccented beat may be used as an embellishment of a triad on the same bass tone. The common tone is held. The other voices move up a 2nd and back.

The tones which form the $\frac{6}{4}$ chord are the upper neighbors of the 3rd and 5th of the triad.

The second inversion of a chord on an unaccented beat may be used as a passing-chord between a triad and its first inversion, or the reverse.

The common tone is held.

One voice, generally the soprano, moves in contrary motion to the bass, using the same three tones in reverse order.

The other voice moves down a 2nd and back.

Drill 19

(1) Fill in the soprano, alto and tenor voices of the following exercises:

(2) Sing the following chords in B♭-major, using the meter and rhythm given on page 20:

$$I \ IV_2 \ I \ I_1 \ IV \ I_2 \ IV_1 \ I_2 \ V \ I$$

$$I \ V_2 \ I_1 \ IV \ IV_2 \ I \ II_1 \ I_2 \ V \ I$$

In b♭-minor:

$$I \ IV \ II_1 \ IV_2 \ I_2 \ V \ VI \ V \ I_2 \ V \ I$$

$$I \ V_2 \ I_1 \ IV \ I_2 \ IV_1 \ I_2 \ VI$$

(3) Fill in the alto and tenor voices of the following exercises:

Any triad in fundamental position may be embellished by a $^6_4$ chord on the same bass tone.   The effect is the expansion of the triad.

The $^6_4$ chord as a passing chord between the triad and its first inversion is used with all triads except the VII and III.   It has the effect of a change from a fundamental chord to its first inversion or the reverse.

There is no sense of progression in either of these uses.

(4) Fill in the alto and tenor voices of the following periods:

(5) Fill in the soprano, alto and tenor voices of the following basses: Work as outlined on pages 22 and 43.

In bass **a,** Measure 1, the figures under the G indicate that G is to be doubled, and in Measure 3 the figures indicate a doubled B♭.

(6)   Harmonize the following melodies:

The $\frac{6}{4}$ preceded and followed by a triad on the same bass tone is used to harmonize the upper neighbor of a tone which is the 5th or 3rd of the triad.

The passing $\frac{6}{4}$ may harmonize the second of any three tones in ascending or descending scale-progression.   This progression is also used to harmonize a tone embellished by its lower neighbor.   This tone is the 8ve of the chord.

Work in the usual way, hearing the general chord-effect and use the $\frac{6}{4}$ chords as embellishments.

(7) Analyze the following excerpt from Mozart Sonata in F-major.

Mozart

(8) Construct original chord-periods in duple and triple meter using Section (4) as a model.

(9) Harmonize the following melodies, using the style of accompaniment given in the model:

With this style of accompaniment the first note of the measure is the bass, the last note a part of the accompaniment. Note that this tone remains in the same register and is either the 5th of the chord or a repetition of the bass.

In the next to the last measure of the model it is not necessary to write in the tones of the V chord.   The ear supplies the resolution of the $\frac{6}{4}$ chord.

(10)   Develop the following motive into a double period:

(11) Invent original motives and develop them into double periods.

LESSON XIX

The bass of a second inversion may move up a 2nd to a fundamental chord.
The doubled tone moves in contrary motion.

The bass of a second inversion may move down a 2nd to a first inversion.
The doubled tone moves in contrary motion.

Drill 20

(1) Fill in the soprano, tenor and alto voices of the following exercises:

(2) Sing the following chords in the key of E-major using the meter and rhythm given on page 20:

$$\text{I VI IV}_1 \text{ I}_2 \text{ IV II}_1 \text{ I}_2 \text{ VI I}_2 \text{ V I}$$

$$\text{I II VI I}_2 \text{ II}_1 \text{ I}_2 \text{ V I IV}_2 \text{ I}$$

In e-minor:

$$\text{I IV II}_1 \text{ I}_2 \text{ IV VI II}_1 \text{ I}_2 \text{ V I}$$

$$\text{I IV V VI I I}_2 \text{ II}_1 \text{ I}_2 \text{ V I}$$

(3) Fill in the alto and tenor voices of the following exercises:
These progressions delay the resolution of the $\frac{6}{4}$ chord and are commonly used for extension.

(4) Fill in the alto and tenor voices of the following periods:

(5) Fill in the soprano, tenor and alto voices of the following basses:

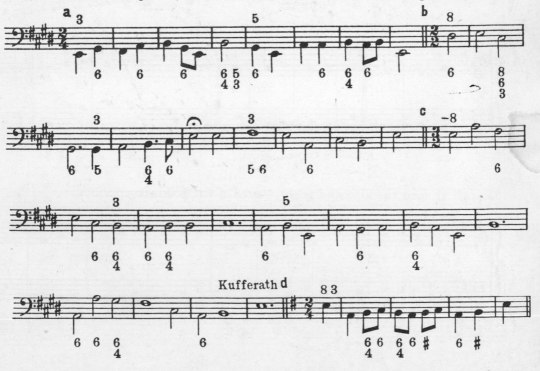

(6)　Harmonize the following melodies:

(7)　Analyze the following piano composition:

The double period may be extended in the same way as the period.　(Review pages 73, 78, 82 and 88.)

All extensions except those at the beginning are best made in the last phrase.

Andante un poco adagio

Mozart

(**8**) Construct original chord-periods in duple and triple meter, using Section (4) as a model.

(**9**) Harmonize the following melodies, using the style of accompaniment given in the model.

A tone that is foreign to the chord and is a part of the next chord is an **anticipation.**

Anticipations are used upon weak pulses or weak sub-divisions of the pulse. (See Measures 6 and **7** of the model.)

Moderato

NOTE. The third tone in Melody 1 is an appoggiatura (see page 133).

(**10**) Develop the following motive into an extended double period.

(**11**) Invent original motives and develop them into extended double periods.

CHAPTER III

SEVENTH-CHORDS

Lesson XX

A 3rd may be added to any triad, forming **a chord of the seventh.**

The figured bass symbols are $_7$, $^7_3$, $^7_5$ or $^8_7$.

The letter and number symbols are G^7 and V^7.

The seventh-chords in common use are:

 The **Augmented Large Seventh**—an augmented triad and a major 7th.

 The **Major Large Seventh**—a major triad and a major 7th.

 The **Minor Large Seventh**—a minor triad and a major 7th.

 The **Dominant Seventh**—a major triad and a minor 7th.

 The **Small Seventh**—a minor triad and a minor 7th.

 The **Half-Diminished Seventh**—a diminished triad and a minor 7th.

 The **Diminished Seventh**—a diminished triad and a diminished 7th.

The seventh-chords used most in a key are the V^7, II^7, IV^7 and VII^7.

The VII^7 is often used in place of the V^7 or V^9 chord because it contains all of the tones of these chords except the root.

The roots of seventh-chords progress in the same way as the roots of triads. The normal resolution is down a 5th.

The V^7 and VII^7 chords progress to the tonic triad.

The other seventh-chords progress to seventh-chords or to a $\frac{6}{4}$ chord representing and followed immediately by a seventh-chord on the same bass tone.

Drill 21

(1)   Fill in the alto and tenor voices of the following chords:

(2)   Fill in the alto and tenor voices of the following chords:
In the V^7 chord the 5th may be omitted and the root doubled.

This doubling occurs in other seventh-chords when used in sequence.
The figured bass symbol for a seventh-chord with doubled root is $\frac{8}{7}$.

The root of a seventh-chord may progress down a 5th to a triad.
The three upper voices move down.

(3) Fill in the soprano, alto and tenor voices of the following chords:

The root of a seventh-chord may progress down a 5th to another seventh-chord.

All three voices move down—or, better,

Keep the common tone;

The other voices move down.

This doubles the root in the second seventh-chord and the 5th is therefore omitted.

(4) Fill in the soprano, alto and tenor voices of the following chords: Each exercise is to be worked in two ways.

When resolving the root of a seventh-chord without a 5th to another seventh-chord:

Keep the common tone;

The other voices move down.

When resolving to a triad:

The 3rd of the chord moves up.

(5) Fill in the soprano, alto and tenor voices of the following chords:

(6) Sing the following chords in the keys of C-major and c-minor, using the meter and rhythm given on page 20:

$$I \ V^7 \ I \ IV \ IV^7 \ II^7 \ V^7 \ I$$

$$I \ VI^7 \ IV^7 \ V^7 \ I \ II^7 \ V^7 \ I$$

$$I \ IV \ II^7 \ I_2 \ V \ VI \ VI^7 \ II^7 \ V^7 \ I$$

$$I \ I_1 \ IV^7 \ II^7 \ I_2 \ V \ I_1 \ IV^7 \ II^7 \ I_2 \ V^7 \ I$$

(7) Fill in the alto and tenor voices of the following exercises:

In hearing seventh-chords the mind first notes the discord, not the individual quality.

In symbolizing, write C^7, G^7, d^7, etc.

The triad quality forming the seventh-chords is figured as usual, capital letters for major triads, small letters for minor triads.

In a major key the I^7 and the IV^7 are large sevenths.

the II^7, III^7 and VI^7 are small sevenths.

the V^7 is a dominant seventh.

the VII^7 is a half diminished seventh.

Exercise **3** would be symbolized C, a^7, d^7, G^7, C.

NOTE. In a minor key, the I^7 is a minor large seventh, the II^7 a half-diminished seventh, the III^7 an augmented large seventh, the IV^7 a small seventh, the V^7 a dominant seventh, the VI^7 a major large seventh, the VII^7 a diminished seventh.

(8) Fill in the alto and tenor voices of the following periods:

(9) Fill in the soprano, alto and tenor voices of the following basses:
    The figures 87 under a bass note, as in bass **a,** Measure 1, indicate that
    the triad is used on the pulse followed by the seventh-chord on the
    subdivision.

(10) Harmonize the following melodies.
    Any tone that resolves diatonically downward may be the seventh of a chord.
    Work in the usual way, first having the sound of the melody firmly fixed in
the mind. Relax and hear the fundamental harmonies underlying the melody.
Note down these harmonies. Next determine which tones in the melody are
chord 7ths. **In this lesson** a 7th may be added to any triad that is progressing
harmonically.

(11) Analyze the following piano composition:

A period may have two antecedent or two consequent phrases. These phrases may be similar or dissimilar.

A group of phrases may be used in place of the period or double-period form.

Two or more independent phrases may be used, each phrase except the last ending with an imperfect authentic cadence or a semi-cadence. The perfect authentic cadence will occur only at the end. These phrases may be similar or dissimilar. If dissimilar, each phrase must be a logical development of the preceding phrase.

(12) Construct original chord-periods in duple and triple meter, using Section (8) as a model.

(13) Harmonize the following melodies, using the style of accompaniment given in the model:

NOTE. Melody **3** is built upon the Aeolian minor scale. Note the B♭ in Measure 2.

(**14**)   Develop the following motive into an extended double-period:

(**15**)   Invent original motives and develop them into extended double-periods.

LESSON XXI

The root of a seventh-chord may progress up a 2nd to a triad or a seventh-chord.

When progressing to a seventh-chord
    The upper voices move down.
When progressing to a triad
    The 3rd of the chord moves up.

The root of a seventh-chord may progress down a 3rd to a seventh-chord, triad or first inversion of a triad.

The 7th of the chord moves up.

Drill 22

(1)   Fill in the soprano, alto and tenor voices of the following chords:

(2) Sing the following chords in the keys of D-major and d-minor, using the meter and rhythm given on page 20:

$$\text{I } V^7 \text{ I}_1 \text{ IV IV}^7 \text{ II}^7 \text{ I}_2 \text{ V}^7 \text{ I}$$

$$\text{I } VI^7 \text{ IV}^7 \text{ II}^7 \text{ V } V^7 \text{ VII}^7 \text{ I}$$

$$\text{I } II^7 \text{ VII}^7 \text{ I IV}_1 \text{ IV}^7 \text{ V}^7 \text{ I}$$

$$\text{I } VII^7 \text{ V}^7 \text{ I II}^7 \text{ I}_2 \text{ V}^7 \text{ I}$$

(3) Fill in the alto and tenor voices of the following exercises:

Test out the sound of each chord before filling in by singing it in arpeggio form from the bass.

Note. In Ex. 4, the progression I-VII⁷ in major, it is necessary to double the 3rd in the I chord so as to prevent consecutive parallel 5ths.

(4) Fill in the alto and tenor voices of the following periods:

(5) Fill in the soprano, alto and tenor voices of the following basses.

In bass **b,** Measure 7, the figures $\frac{7}{5}\frac{5}{7}$ under the E indicate that one voice will progress from the 7th to the 5th of the chord and another voice from the 5th to the 7th.

(6) Harmonize the following melodies:

A tone which ascends diatonically may be the 7th of a chord whose root moves down a 3rd.

(7) Analyze the following piano composition:

A composition is often divided into two contrasting sections, because of a perfect authentic cadence in the middle.

That is a **two-part form.**

Each part may be a phrase, a period or a group of two or more phrases.

Part II generally has new melodic material, and is often contrasting in style, yet must give the feeling of a continuation of Part I.

This differs from the period and double-period forms because of the perfect authentic cadence in the middle.

Part I may end at a perfect authentic cadence in the key of the dominant, if the composition is in major, and with a perfect authentic cadence in the relative major key, if in minor.   Until Lesson 28 these examples will not modulate.

Martini

(8)   Construct original chord-periods in duple and triple meter, using Section (4) as a model.

(9)   Harmonize the following melodies, using the style of accompaniment given in the model:

This style of accompanying a folk-song uses three and four voices, alternating between close and open position according to which is more playable.

Andante

Folk - Song

1

Folk - Song

2

Folk-Song 3

Old - Song 4

(10) Develop the following motive into a two-part song form, using Sections (7) and (9) as models:

Andante

mf

(11) Invent original motives and develop them into two-part song forms.

Lesson XXII

The root of a seventh-chord may progress up a 2nd to a first inversion, or down a 4th to a seventh-chord, triad or first inversion of a triad.

The chord 7th remains stationary.

Upon weak pulses or sub-divisions of pulses the chord 7th may progress to the nearest chord tones before resolving.

The other voices remain stationary.

Drill 23

(1) Fill in the soprano, alto and tenor voices of the following chords:

(2) Sing the following chords in the key of B♭-major, using the meter and rhythm given on page 20.

$$\text{I V}^7\text{ IV}_1\text{ V}^7\text{ I}_1\text{ II II}^7\text{ I}_2\text{ V}^7\text{ I}$$

$$\text{I V}^7\text{ VI IV}^7\text{ V}^7\text{ II V}^7\text{ I}$$

In b♭-minor:

$$\text{I I}_1\text{ IV II}^7\text{ V}^7\text{ IV}_1\text{ I}$$

$$\text{I II}_1\text{ V}^7\text{ IV}_1\text{ IV II}^7\text{ V}^7\text{ I}$$

(3) Fill in the alto and tenor voices of the following exercises:

In Exercises 6, 7 and 8, on the second half of the pulses which have seventh-chords, the chord 7th moves up, changing the chord to a triad. But as the ear retains the sound of the chord 7th the entire pulse is considered a seventh-chord. **The resolution of the chord seventh is said to be delayed.**

(4) Fill in the alto and tenor voices of the following periods: Take from dictation when possible, otherwise play the soprano and the bass several times, hearing the chord quality.

(5) Fill in the soprano, alto and tenor voices of the following basses: Sing the chords in arpeggio form from these basses.

(6) Harmonize the following melodies. Memorize the melody before harmonizing, determining the general chord-effect.

The first progression given in this lesson will be found useful in harmonizing repeated tones, and in postponing the resolution of a seventh-chord.

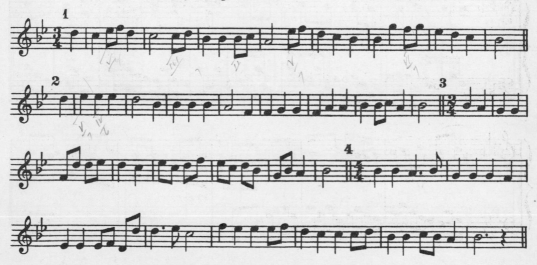

(**7**)   Analyze the following piano composition:

A two-part form may be extended at the beginning with an introduction.

It may be extended at the end of Parts I and II by any of the extension means used in the preceding lessons, also by a **codetta.**

A codetta is generally two measures in length, uses the chords of the cadence, and contains some outstanding melodic material from the composition.

Mendelssohn

(8) Construct original chord-periods, using Section (4) as a model.

(9) Harmonize the following folk-songs for voice and piano, using the style of accompaniment given in the model.

Note that only three tones of each chord are used in the accompaniment.

In the melody the notes are not beamed because each word and syllable must have a separate note. If two or three tones are sung to one vowel-sound, the notes are beamed as in Exercise (1), Measure 2.

NOTE FOR MELODY 2. Because of the character of this song, use quarter-notes in the accompaniment in place of the eighth-note and eighth-rest.

Folk-Song

(10) Develop the following motive into an extended two-part song-form, making a setting for voice and piano of the following nursery rhyme:

Pease porridge hot,
    Pease porridge cold,
Pease porridge in the pot,
    Nine days old.

Some like it hot,
    Some like it cold,
Some like it in the pot,
    Nine days old.

(11) Invent original motives and develop them into extended two-part song-forms.

CHAPTER IV

THE INVERSION OF SEVENTH-CHORDS

LESSON XXIII

There are three inversions of seventh-chords: the first inversion with the 3rd of the chord in the bass; the second inversion with the 5th of the chord in the bass: the third inversion with the 7th of the chord in the bass.

The figured bass symbol for a 1st inversion is $^6_5$, 2nd inversion $^4_3$, and 3rd inversion $^4_2$.

The letter and numeral symbols are:

For 1st Inversion G^6_5 or G^7_1, and V_6 or V^7_1.

For 2nd Inversion G^4_3 or G^7_2, and V_4 or V^7_2.

For 3rd Inversion G^4_2 or G^7_3, and V_4 or V^7_3.

In giving the specific quality of an inverted seventh-chord, i.e., if it is diminished or half diminished, use the quality sign given in the preceding lessons.

For example, this chord would be symbolized $g^{ø4}_3$

Seventh-chords are inverted to give diatonic bass progressions. Also to give a feeling of pulse in chord repetition.

No tone is doubled or omitted in the inversions of seventh-chords.

In resolving the inversions of seventh-chords to triads or seventh-chords:
  The 3rd of the chord moves up to the root of the chord of resolution;
  The common tone is held;
  The remaining voices move down.

Drill 24

THE FIRST INVERSION OF SEVENTH-CHORDS

The bass of a first inversion of a seventh-chord will move up a 2nd to the root of a triad or of a seventh-chord. A $\frac{6}{4}$ chord may be substituted for a fundamental chord.

(1) Fill in the soprano, alto and tenor voices of the following chords:

(2) Sing the following chords in the keys of G-major and g-minor, using the meter and rhythm given on page 20.

$$\text{I } V^7 \ V_1^7 \ \text{I } \text{IV } II^7 \ II_1^7 \ V^7 \ \text{I}$$
$$\text{I } VI^7 \ IV^7 \ II_1^7 \ I_2 \ V^7 \ \text{I}$$
$$\text{I } V_1^7 \ \text{I } \text{IV } II_1^7 \ V^7 \ \text{I}$$
$$\text{I } II_1^7 \ V \ VI \ VI^7 \ IV^7 \ II_1^7 \ V^7 \ V_1^7 \ \text{I}$$

(3) Fill in the alto and tenor voices of the following exercises:

The first inversion of seventh-chords is in effect like an embellishment of the fundamental chord to which it resolves.

The first inversion of the V^7 and II^7 are most used, the first inversion of the V^7 as an embellishment of the I, the II^7 as an embellishment of the V. The II_1^7 is often used as a substitute for the I_2 or a repeated dominant.

The first inversion of seventh-chords is determined in dictation by the diatonic resolution of the bass up a 2nd to a fundamental chord. It is easily recognized when preceded by a fundamental chord on the same bass tone.

Note in Ex. 6, the exceptional resolution of the VII_5^6 chord up a 2nd to the I_6 chord.

(4) Fill in the alto and tenor voices of the following periods:

(5) Fill in the soprano, alto and tenor voices of the following basses: Sing the chords in arpeggio form from these basses.

(6) Harmonize the following melodies, using first inversions of seventh-chords whenever possible:

(7) Analyze the following piano composition:

Andante con moto

Beethoven

(8) Construct original chord-periods in duple and triple meter, using Section (4) as a model.

(9) Harmonize the following melodies using the style of accompaniment given in the model.

A melody may skip from below to the upper neighbor and from above to the lower neighbor of a chord-tone. This neighboring tone will resolve immediately to the chord-tone.

A neighboring tone which is preceded by a skip is called an **appoggiatura.**

In harmonizing a melody the ear is the safest guide in determining the appoggiatura.

Andantino

(10) Develop the following motive into a two-part song-form:

(11) Invent original motives and develop them into two-part song-forms.

Lesson XXIV
THE SECOND AND THIRD INVERSIONS OF SEVENTH-CHORDS

The bass of a second inversion of a seventh-chord resolves down a 2nd to a fundamental triad or seventh-chord.

The bass of a third inversion of a seventh-chord resolves down a 2nd to the first inversion of a triad or seventh-chord, or to a fundamental seventh-chord.

Drill 25

(1) Fill in the soprano, alto and tenor voices of the following chords:

The dominant seventh in the second inversion may be used as a passing-chord between the tonic and its first inversion or the reverse.

The 7th of the chord moves in 3rds with the bass.

The 5th is generally doubled in the I_1.

In resolving a seventh-chord in the third inversion, the 5th or the root of the chord may jump up a 4th.

The fundamental position and successive inversions of the same seventh-chord may be used in any order.   If the third inversion resolves up to the fundamental chord, the chord 7th is omitted and the bass moves down a 3rd to a first inversion.   This is the delayed resolution in the bass of the chord 7th.   (See Drill 23.)

(2)   Sing the following chords in the key of A-flat major.

$$I \; V \; V^7 \; I \; II^7 \; V^7_2 \; I$$

$$I \; II^7_3 \; V^7_1 \; I \; VI \; II^7_2 \; V^7 \; I$$

$$I \; V^7_2 \; I_1 \; II^7_1 \; V^7_3 \; IV^7 \; I_2 \; V^7 \; I$$

$$I \; II^7 \; II^7_1 \; II^7_2 \; V^7 \; V^7_3 \; V^7_2 \; V^7_1 \; I$$

(3)   Fill in the alto and tenor voices of the following exercises:
Note the following effects in the use of these progressions.
For the I V^7_2 I$_1$ and the reverse, the harmonic effect is the tonic chord changing through passing-tones to its first inversion.
The I V^7_3 I$_1$ is also a change from the tonic to its first inversion.
The $^4_2$, preceded by a triad on the same bass tone, is a suspension in the bass. The $^4_2$, preceded by the root position of the same chord, is a passing-tone in the bass.

(4)   Fill in the alto and tenor voices of the following periods:

Bach

(5) Fill in the soprano, alto and tenor voices of the following basses: Hear mentally the quality of each chord and sing the chords in arpeggio form from these basses.

(6) Harmonize the following melodies, using all inversions of seventh-chords:

Harmonize the melodic progression 3-4-5 with the I V$_3^4$ I$_6$; the skips 2-5 and 5-8 with the V$_2^4$ I$_6$.

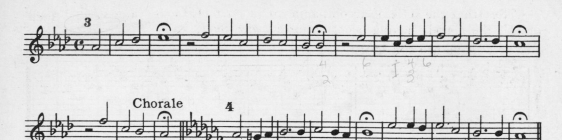

Chorale

(7) Analyze the following piano composition:

A composition which is divided into three sections, the third section a return to the first, is a **Three-Part Form** (A.B.A.).

Part I may be a phrase, period, double-period or group of phrases. The cadence at the end of Part I may be a perfect authentic cadence in the original key, in the key of the dominant, if in major, or in the relative major key, if in minor. Part I is often repeated.

Part II may be any form, is contrasting to Part I, and generally uses new melodic and harmonic material, but must be a logical continuation and development of Part I.

The cadence of Part II is generally made upon the V chord of the original key.

The third part must begin and continue as in Part I for at least two measures. It may be an exact or modified repetition of Part I.

Parts II and III are generally repeated together.

When each part is only a phrase in length, the form is a **Three-Part Period.**

Con Spirito

Folk - Song

(8) Construct original chord-periods in duple and triple meter, using Section (4) as a model.

(9) Harmonize the following melodies, using the style of accompaniment given in the model:

Note that the style of accompaniment in Part III is the same as in Parts I and II, the melody having been reinforced with 8ves.

(**10**)   Develop the following motive into a three-part period.

Andante con moto

(**11**)   Invent original motives, and develop them into three-part periods.

Lesson XXV

SEVENTH-CHORDS AND INVERSIONS (*Continued*)

Drill 26

(**1**)   Sing the following chords in the key of F-major and f-minor, according to the meter and rhythm given on page 20:

$$\text{I VI IV}_1^7\ \text{I}_2\ \text{V}^7\ \text{V}_3^7\ \text{I}_1\ \text{II}_1^7\ \text{I}_2\ \text{V}^7\ \text{I}$$

$$\text{I II}_3^7\ \text{VII}^7\ \text{V}_1^7\ \text{II}_2^7\ \text{II}_1^7\ \text{I}_2\ \text{V}^7\ \text{I}$$

(**2**)   Fill in the alto and tenor voices of the following exercises:

Note.   The bass of the IV_1^7 may resolve down a 2nd to the I_2.   Ex. 5.

(**3**)   Fill in the alto and tenor voices of the following exercises:

In the Folk-Song, Exercise **4**, note that in the first phrase there is one chord to a measure, in the second phrase, two chords.   In a folk-song of this type it is not necessary to change the bass for each repeated tone, as the repeated tone is unessential.

Folk - Song

(4) Fill in the soprano, alto and tenor of the following basses:

NOTE.   In bass **a,** the figures in parenthesis in Measure 7 are passing-tones.

Largo (transposed)   Haydn Op. 33, No. 2

(5) Harmonize the following folk-songs:

(6) Analyze the following piano composition:

A three-part period may be extended at the beginning with an introduction:

At the end of Part I with an evasion of the cadence or the repetition of the cadence chords:

At the end of Part II with an evasion or the expansion of the cadence:

At the end of Part III in all ways.

In the course of any phrase by the repetition or sequence of a motive. (Example on page 59.)

(7) Construct original chord-periods in duple and triple meter, using Section (3) as a model.

(8) Harmonize the following folk-songs for voice and piano, using any style of accompaniment from the preceding lessons that may seem to be appropriate.

(9) Develop the following motive into an extended three-part period.

(10) Invent original motives and develop them into extended three-part periods.

CHAPTER V
NINTH-CHORDS
LESSON XXVI

A 3rd may be added to a seventh-chord forming a chord of the 9th.

Symbolized G^9, V^9
In four-part harmony the 5th of the chord is omitted.

G^9

Drill 27

(1) Fill in the alto and tenor voices of the following chords:

The root of a ninth-chord may resolve down a 5th to a triad.
The 3rd of the chord moves up.
The other voices move down.
A ninth-chord may be followed by a seventh-chord on the same bass tone.
The 9th resolves down.
In all other progressions of the root of a ninth-chord the 3rd moves up, or
if it is a common tone it remains stationary.

(2) Fill in the soprano, alto and tenor of the following chords:

Ninth-chords are seldom inverted in four-part harmony.

The 9th of the chord is generally in the soprano.

The most used ninth-chords are the V^9 and II^9 in major, the V^9 and IV^9 in minor.

(3) Sing the following chords in arpeggio form. In singing a ninth-chord change the rhythm to

In E-major:

$$I\ VI^7\ IV^7\ II^9\ V^7\ V^9\ VII^7\ I$$
$$I\ I_1\ II^9\ II^7\ V^7\ V^7_1\ I\ V^9\ VII^7\ I$$

In e-minor:

$$I\ IV^7\ IV^9\ II^7_1\ V^9\ V^9\ I$$
$$I\ VII^7\ I\ VI^7\ IV^9\ I_2\ V^9\ V^7\ I$$

(4) Fill in the alto and tenor voices of the following exercises:

The ninth-chord in most uses sounds like a suspension or a neighbor of the seventh-chord on the same bass tone.

(5) Fill in the alto and tenor voices of the following periods. Sing each of the chords in arpeggio form before filling in.

(6) Fill in the soprano, alto and tenor of the following basses:

(7) Harmonize the following melodies, using ninth-chords whenever possible:

(8)   Analyze the following piano composition:

Part I of a three-part form may be a period, Part II a phrase and Part III a phrase, a reduction of Part I.   This is called an **Incipient Three-Part Form.**

Each part may be extended in the usual manner.

Beethoven

(9) Construct original chord-periods in duple and triple meter using Section (5) as a model.

(10) Harmonize the following melodies using the style of accompaniment given in the model:

Allegro

(11) Develop the following motive into an incipient three-part form:

(12) Invent original motives and develop them into incipient three-part forms.

CHAPTER VI

MODULATION

A composition for the piano or violin, a song or a symphony is in a tonality. One speaks of the C-sharp Prelude, a Symphony in D minor.

This feeling of tonality is a natural phenomenon, and once a tonality is set up it is unconsciously retained in the mind of the listener throughout the composition. Many of the laws which govern the technique of composition are the result of the demand for the preservation of tonality.

There is a wealth of harmonic color in a given tonality secured by the use of triads, seventh-chords, ninth-chords and inversions, as given in this book, and in chromatic and embellishing harmony in Book II.

It is also possible to expand any chord in the key by temporarily treating this chord as a key-center and resolving chords into it. This is known as **modulation.** This establishing of a new center does not upset the feeling of the original tonality.

Modulations are used in large compositions, such as sonatas and symphonies and in part-forms for contrasting subjects and parts. In the first movement of a sonata in a major key, the second subject is generally in the key of the dominant. In the three-part song-form the second part may be in the key of the dominant. In small forms such as the two-part song-form, the period and the double-period, a modulation may be made at a cadence and the composition continued for several chords in the new key. A perfect authentic cadence must be used, otherwise it will sound like dominant or diminished seventh embellishments. (See Lessons I and IV, Book II.)

Any of the diatonic harmonies except the VII may be set up as a new key-center; i.e., a modulation may be made to the key of the dominant, sub-dominant, mediant, super-tonic, sub-mediant. It is not customary to modulate before the tonality of the composition has been established.

LESSON XXVII

A new key may be entered through the V^7 and any of its inversions, also **through the VII^7.**

The key from which the modulation is made ends with the I chord (or sometimes the VI chord).

In entering the new key the I_6^4 may be substituted for the V^7.

It is necessary to continue for three or more chords in the new key in order to establish the change of tonality.

After a cadence a new phrase may begin with the I chord of a new key.

Bach

In the above chorale, phrase 1 establishes the key of E-major.

Phrase 2 modulates to the key of c-sharp minor through the b-sharp diminished chord in Measure 4.

Phrase 3 modulates to B-major through the $F\#^6_5$ chord.

Phrase 4 begins in E-major. The B-major chord at the cadence of phrase 3 is heard and treated as both the I chord of B-major and the V chord of E-major.

Drill 28

(1)   Fill in the alto and tenor voices of the following exercises:

These exercises are different processes of progressing from the tonic of one key to the tonic of another.

(2) Using the exercises under Section (1) as models, modulate from each major and minor key to all the keys represented by the diatonic harmony.

(3) Sing the following chords in the key of C-major:

C-maj.	G-maj.
I V⁷ I	V⁷ I₂ V⁷ I

C-maj.	F-maj.
I V⁷₁ I	V⁷₁ I V⁷ I

C-maj.	d-min.
I II⁷ V⁷ I	VII⁷ I V⁷ I

C-maj.	e-min.
I V⁷₂ I	V⁷ VII⁷ I

C-maj.	a-min.
I V⁷ I	V⁷₃ I₁ V⁷₂ I

(4) Fill in the alto and tenor voices of the following exercises. Hear the quality of each chord and test it by singing the chord in arpeggio form.

After the student has marked the letter-name and quality of the chord, he should mark the scale-degrees of the soprano; e.g., No. 1 is 8 8 2 8 7 8 2 8. If the last two tones A G are 2 8, the key must be G-major and the chords V⁷ I.

In some cases the soprano will be heard as a scale-degree in both keys; e.g., in No. 1 of Section 5, the C at the end of Measure 2 is first heard as the eighth degree of C, and then as the mind reflects it is also heard as the fourth degree of G-major.

(5) Harmonize the following excerpts from chorales. Analyze. Mark the keys to which the modulations are made.

NOTE. When giving these exercises in dictation, work in the usual manner. In these chorales the student may reverse the order and write the soprano first.

(6) Fill in the soprano, alto and tenor voices of the following basses:

Be sure that the quality of each chord is heard mentally. When not certain, stop and sing the chord in arpeggio form.

Mark the keys, symbolize the chords and the scale-degrees in the soprano.

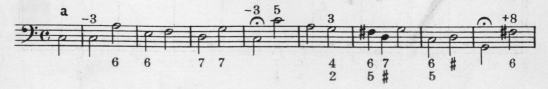

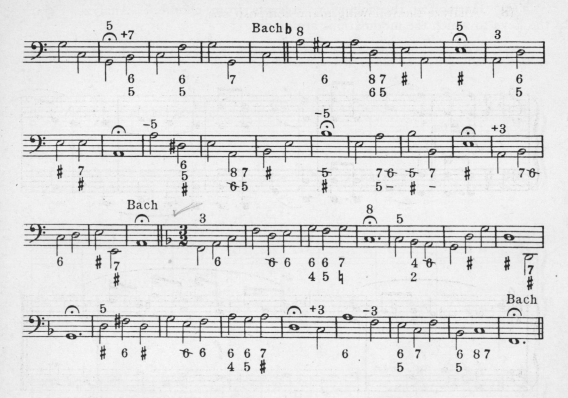

(7) Harmonize the following melodies:

First memorize the sound of the melody.

Next analyze any change of key. Determine exactly at what point the modulation occurs, remembering that the key will close with some tone of the I or VI chords.

In some places where modulations are not obvious in sound, analyze the possibilities.

(8) Analyze the following piano composition:

Schubert

(9) Harmonize the following melodies for violin and piano, using the style of accompaniment given in the model:

Note that in this style of accompaniment the 3rd is not doubled in the major chords, and that the right hand is the harmonic background in close position.

Hauptman, arr.

(**10**) Develop the following motive into an incipient three-part song-form.

(**11**) Invent original motives and develop them into incipient three-part song-forms.

Lesson XXVIII

A modulation to any of the keys represented by the diatonic chords may be made through the VI, IV and II^7 chords and inversions.

The key from which the modulation is made ends with the I chord or VI chord.

Drill 29

(1) Fill in the alto and tenor voices of the following exercises:

(2) Using the above exercises as models, modulate from each major and minor key to all keys represented by the diatonic harmony.

(3) Sing the following chords in the key of F-major.

F-maj.   C-maj.
$\overline{\text{I V}^7_1 \text{ I}}$ $\overline{\text{II}^7_1 \text{ I}_2 \text{ V}^7 \text{ I}}$

F-maj.   Bb-maj.
$\overline{\text{I V}^7 \text{ I}}$ $\overline{\text{V}^7_3 \text{ I}_1 \text{ V}^7_2 \text{ I}}$

F-maj.   d-min.
$\overline{\text{I V}^9 \text{ I}}$ $\overline{\text{II}^7_1 \text{ I}_2 \text{ V}^7 \text{ I}}$

F-maj.   g-min.
$\overline{\text{I VII}^7 \text{ I}}$ $\overline{\text{II}^7_2 \text{ I}_2 \text{ V}^7 \text{ I}}$

(4) Fill in the alto and tenor voices of the following exercises according to instructions given in the preceding lesson.

(5) Harmonize the following excerpts from chorales.

NOTE. In these exercises some of the beats are sub-divided with passing-tones which form seventh- and six-four chords. The principal harmonies should be indicated first, the passing harmonies later. No. 1 would be Eb Ab6 Eb Bb.

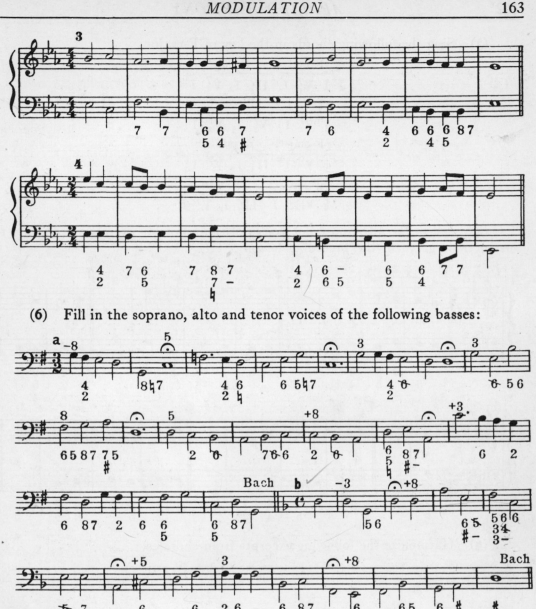

(6) Fill in the soprano, alto and tenor voices of the following basses:

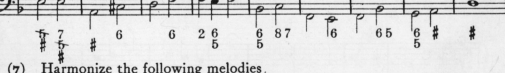

(7) Harmonize the following melodies.

Mendelssohn

(8)   Analyze the following piano composition:

Schubert

Fine

(9)   Harmonize the following folk-songs either for piano solo or for voice with piano accompaniment:

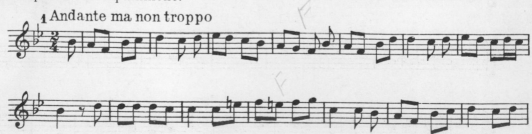

(10)   Develop the following motive into an incipient three-part song-form:

Allegro con moto

(11)   Invent original motives and develop them into incipient three-part song-forms.